The Theme Immersion Compendium for Social Studies Teaching

MARYANN MANNING
GARY MANNING
ROBERTA LONG

HEINEMANN
Portsmouth, NH

Heinemann
A Division of Reed Elsevier Inc.
361 Hanover Street
Portsmouth, NH 03801-3912

Offices and agents throughout the world

Library of Congress Cataloging-in-Publication Data
Manning, Maryann Murphy.
    The theme immersion compendium for social studies teaching /
Maryann Manning, Gary Manning, Roberta Long.
        p.   cm.
    Includes bibliographical references.
    ISBN 0–435–08884–X (acid-free paper)
    1. Social sciences—Study and teaching (Elementary)—United
States.   2. Social sciences—Study and teaching (Middle school)—
United States.   I. Manning, Gary L.   II. Long, Roberta.
III. Title.
LB1584.M29   1997
372.83 043—dc21   96–53523
                                                         CIP

Editors: Carolyn Coman and William Varner
Production: Melissa L. Inglis
Cover design: Jenny Jensen Greenleaf
Cover photo: Clark Underbakke
Manufacturing: Louise Richardson

Printed in the United States of America on acid-free paper
00 99 98 97   RRD   1 2 3 4 5 6 7 8 9

4/23/98

Contents

Introduction

A number of teachers who have read and used our book, *Theme Immersion: Inquiry-Based Curriculum in Elementary and Middle Schools*, say the book truly helps them as they implement themes in their elementary and middle school classrooms. They tell us that the lists of resources in the back of the book are especially helpful, and wish for more. These teachers do not want teacher-directed theme books that dictate curriculum, but they want help in identifying resources.

We were further encouraged to develop this because of recommendations made by various professional groups. The National Council of Teachers of Social Studies, for example, stresses that students in elementary grades should engage in integrated themes and that all social studies should be integrated. In one of its documents, *Curriculum Standards for the Social Studies* (1994), the council states, "Social studies programs should reflect the changing nature of knowledge, fostering entirely new and highly integrated approaches to resolving issues of significance to humanity" (5). In addition to stressing the importance of themes, the document emphasizes the need for students to construct a more personal, pluralistic, and global perspective.

In response to these expressions of concern, we provide this resource book. The book is not prescriptive, but rather is intended to support teachers who implement theme immersions. We selected the broad categories of conflict, settlement of the United States, global awareness, and cultural diversity within the United States because they encompass many areas studied in elementary and middle schools.

In Chapter 1, we provide a brief overview of the theme immersion process, which is explained in detail in our earlier book on theme immersion. Chapters 2 through 5 include numerous suggestions and resources for studying each broad topic. We suggest questions that might be used as students consider what they want to know about a topic and subtopics that relate to the questions. We list resources for studying the topic and suggest ways for students to express their knowledge about the topic. In the appendices, many ideas are proposed, such as forms for evaluation.

A brief discussion is included for each step of the theme immersion (TI) process for the first TI in each section. Suggestions for the TIs that follow are in outline form.

Acknowledgments

It is not possible to acknowledge all the friends and colleagues who made contributions to this book. If we were to do so, this section would be longer than the book itself. However, we do wish to give our sincere thanks to the following educators who helped in some way: Sharon Bounds, Joy Burrows, Sonia Carrington, Shelly Chumley, Susan Johnston, Linda Maxwell, Brian McElhaney, Gayle Morrison, Patricia Nix, Mary-Martha Rhodes, Donna Salmon, Cecil Teague, Dottie Thompson, and Clark Underbakke.

We also want to thank our colleagues at our university for their assistance: Bobbie Booker, Richard Cecil, Constance Kamii, Ed Ort, Paul Pedersen, Fran Perkins, Cecilia Pierce, and JoAnn Portalupi.

We offer a special thanks to our colleague Lois Christensen, who responded to the manuscript in its entirety and added many useful resources. We are indebted to Smith Williams, who shared his professional library on multicultural literature with us. Further, we appreciate Ivan Kelava and Virginia Lynn, who assisted us in the final phases of the book.

We will always be appreciative of Pat Broderick, vice president of *Teaching K–8*, and Philippa Stratton, former Heinemann editor in chief, who were instrumental in the publication of the parent book, *Theme Immersion: Inquiry-Based Curriculum in Elementary and Middle Schools*. Carolyn Coman, our first editor for this book, gave us valuable guidance in the creation of the manuscript. We also thank Bill Varner, the current editor, for his helpful assistance.

Finally, we are deeply grateful to family members Delbert Long, husband of Roberta, for his unending support; and Marilee Roberta Manning, the daughter of the Mannings, whose patience and love were a source of comfort and encouragement to us.

Maryann Manning, Gary Manning, and Roberta Long

Overview of the Theme Immersion Process

The process of *theme immersion* (TI) is explained in our earlier book, *Theme Immersion: Inquiry-Based Curriculum in Elementary and Middle Schools*. Figure 1–1 shows the elements of this process: select topic; make lists and web; form study committees; develop questions; study topic; express knowledge; and assess and evaluate. In the following pages, we briefly review the process.

Select Topic

If students are to become truly immersed in a topic of study, the topic must be of interest to them and should be important to the classroom community and to society at large. In addition, it must be broad enough in scope to help students develop an awareness of the interconnectedness of and knowledge of the world.

In our dream school, the students and the teacher are ecstatic about all the topics that are studied, but we know that is only a dream. More success will be achieved, however, if all voices are represented in the selection of a topic and if there is ample latitude for pursuing various aspects of the theme. Some topics are chosen by the students, others by the teacher, or a topic may flow naturally from a shared class experience. Then, of course, there are topics that may be mandated by the school system or state department of education (see Figure 1–2).

Make Lists and Web

Begin by asking students to make lists of their knowledge about a topic and possible areas of interest. We suggest that their ideas be categorized

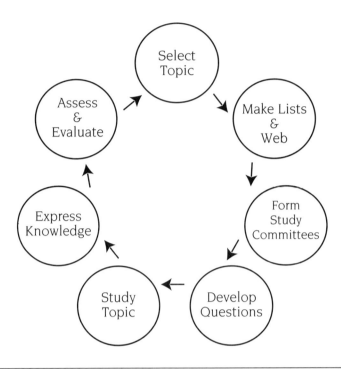

Figure 1–1

under two headings: "What we know" and "What we want to know." For example, if the topic is "Jamestown to Independence in 1783," the students might say that they know: the Pilgrims settled at Jamestown, the thirteen colonies were developed during this time period, the colonists declared their independence from England, and the colonists fought against England during the Revolutionary War. When identifying what they want to know, the students might ask: Why did people come to America? Who were the Pilgrims? What were Britain's reasons for wanting the colonies? Where were the early settlements? What political, social, and religious beliefs did the colonists hold?

After the questions have been completed, the students identify subtopics that represent the questions. It is important to remember that one question often relates to more than one subtopic.

TI teachers and their students then construct a web of the subtopics and continue to brainstorm ideas related to the subtopics. The teacher usually uses the chalkboard for webbing, erasing as students change their minds and observe new relationships. The final web is then copied from the chalkboard onto a large piece of butcher or

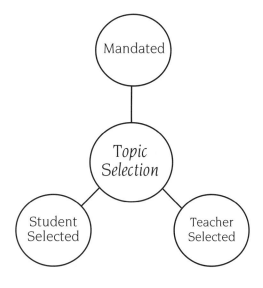

FIGURE 1–2

poster paper so that the class can refer to it throughout the TI. Figure 1–3 shows a web developed by one class.

Form Study Committees

After completing a web, the students need to be organized into study committees. The teacher asks the students to decide with whom and how they want to study. Do they want to work in a group with three or four others? What topics do they prefer to research? How are they going to engage in their research?

When students identify their choices, the teacher notes their preferences. At least two students work on the same subtopic. Balancing group choices can be difficult, but teachers are usually able to group everyone with at least one classmate preference.

Develop Questions

After committees are formed, each committee develops questions related to the subtopic and then records them on a blank transparency so they can be shared with the large group. After reading their questions aloud to the class, the students ask for responses from the class, such

FIGURE 1–3

as "Do all of the questions make sense and do they sound interesting?" "Does anyone have questions to add?" "Should any questions be deleted?" "Do you have any suggestions to offer us?"

Study Topic

Students begin their research. The teacher serves as a facilitator and a guide. TI teachers move from group to group, individual to individual, guiding students as they find answers to their questions and helping them assess their individual and group research strategies and their group processes. They help students clarify their ideas, look for resources, and locate resource people. When teachers note a problem or recognize an individual or group need, they issue an invitation to a demonstration lesson or a guided engagement session.

The class uses a variety of information sources (see Appendix E), including books and other print sources; resource people and media; and real objects and experiences. In this book, the annotated fiction and nonfiction books are classified at one of the following three levels: P = primary level (grades 1–3); I = intermediate level (grades 4–6); and MS = middle school level (grades 7–8). Needless to say, these classifications are not meant to be interpreted rigidly.

Teachers also participate in research, and this infusion of content from the teacher inspires students and extends their knowledge base. Students share information they find that may be of help to other individual students or groups. When the teacher or a group of students finds a community resource person, other students may be invited to hear the speaker even though the topic may not be directly related to what they are researching. Likewise, if anyone finds media that relate to one group's question, other students are often invited to view or listen to that particular film, video, or tape.

As students become independent researchers, various research techniques, such as notetaking and interviewing, are used to collect information. Teachers facilitate students' research skills through demonstrations. For instance, the teacher might read a selection from a text in front of the students and show them how to take notes. They make their notes on the chalkboard or on an overhead and talk about what they're doing and why they selected particular points to record.

In order to develop students' ability to conduct effective interviews, TI teachers demonstrate interviewing techniques. As they plan to interview a guest who will speak to the class, the teacher puts some questions she wants to ask on the board and the students add to the list. To focus inquiry during the interview, the teacher and the students select the most important questions and put them on note cards (see the interview ideas in Chapters 2 through 5).

Before the speaker visits the class, the students discuss other aspects of the interview. They might decide to tape-record the interview if the guest doesn't object, so they can review the tape later to make sure they don't miss any important points. When the guest arrives, the teacher introduces the person to the class and begins the interview by asking a question. Members of the class and the teacher intersperse their questions throughout the interview. In this way, students gain experience in how to conduct an interview. They learn interviewing procedures through an authentic encounter, not by going over these procedures simply to learn how to interview. Later, the teacher and the students transcribe parts of the interview and talk about how to organize the information. The students are now ready to use the interview technique independently as one means of gathering information (see Appendix E).

Express Knowledge

TI teachers want students to express their knowledge in a great number of ways and for different purposes (see Appendix E). This diversity is important because it taps the creative powers of students who learn in different ways, and who express what they learn in different ways, reflecting their own emotional, intellectual, and imaginative powers. There are, of course, many forms for expression in TIs. Possibilities include the visual arts, construction projects, dramatization, speaking, movement, music, writing, and technology.

Assess and Evaluate

In TIs, students investigate questions that relate to a particular topic. With guidance from the teacher, they select questions to explore, locate and use a variety of resources, and report their findings. The teacher uses these activities in the assessment and evaluation of students during the TI. Assessment consists of the data gathered by students, teachers, and parents. Students accumulate their data in files and create portfolios of their best efforts. Teachers keep records of students' growth and development, and parents, too, contribute information about their children's learning. Needless to say, assessment and evaluation are a challenge for most teachers; TI teachers truly involve students in the assessment and evaluation process with an emphasis on self-evaluation. While some TI teachers would like to eliminate grading, they are still required to assign a letter or percentage grade on student reports. If you are faced with this dilemma, you may have to give a little to keep a lot.

It's a struggle to move toward more meaningful evaluation, especially when many teachers are still expected to administer traditional tests and assign a grade, but it is a struggle worth making. We are all continuing to seek ways to interpret students' efforts so that our means of assessment and evaluation are educationally sound enough to successfully challenge those currently being used. In Appendix C, we provide several forms for assessment, evaluation, and grading.

The student's file contains everything the student and the teacher want to save: drafts of reports, notes, summaries, outlines, logs, and journals. It is a repository of student work and expands as the year progresses. Students can reserve one section of their file for works in progress and another for completed, polished work. In addition to their own work, students might also include the group or individual reporting forms and checklists they complete during and after TIs.

In addition to a file, each student has a TI portfolio. While the file contains everything the student and the teacher want saved, the portfolio contains work carefully selected by the student, which includes materials from the file. The organization of a portfolio varies; it can be organized chronologically according to topic or type of material. Students include notes from their oral presentations and summaries of texts they have read as well as texts they have written. If done well, a portfolio increases students' self-confidence; they take pride in the work they place in a portfolio because it shows their progress and development. The portfolio also allows the teacher and the parents to evaluate students' work.

Conflicts
  - individually
Group Conflicts
  - classmates
  - Martin Luther King Jr.
Military conflicts
  - Desert Storm
  - Current Events.

Conflict

2

Time + Kids.com

Human conflict stirs strong emotional responses, especially when it results in violence. Unfortunately, we see violence all too often. It often fills the television or radio. Newscasts sensationally report violent actions such as horrible crimes, military actions, and stories about violence, many a result of discrimination and inequalities at home and abroad. Students have personal experiences with conflict, and some have firsthand experience with violent conflict in their own homes and communities.

When people perceive a difference between their interests and the interests of others, conflict may occur. These perceived differences occur between individuals, groups, and nations. There are many sources of interpersonal conflict, including inequality of resources, differences in values and beliefs, and differences in the way people perceive their roles in relationships.

In this section, we present resources for TIs on interpersonal conflict, intergroup conflict, and military conflict. In addition to the general TI on military conflict, we provide several TIs on specific military conflicts, such as the Revolutionary War.

Select Topic: Interpersonal Conflict

Conflict, a form of social interaction in school and in the community, can contribute to the social and emotional development of individuals. However, if people do not know how to engage in conflict appropriately and resolve their conflict in satisfactory ways, violence or other negative outcomes may occur. Unfortunately, violence in the United States has increased significantly. Therefore, educators, parents, and others must take an active role in helping individuals learn how to settle or resolve their conflict in appropriate ways.

Make Lists and Web

If you and your students have selected the topic "Interpersonal Conflict," the next step is to assess your students' prior knowledge by asking them to tell what they know about interpersonal conflict. We suggest a whole-class brainstorming session where you make a list of what they know on a transparency or on the chalkboard. After this list is completed, encourage the class to ask questions about what they would like to know. The following may help you and your students as you make your own lists of "What we want to know."

What We Want to Know

- What is conflict?
- Does everyone disagree with someone else once in a while?
- Can you disagree with someone and still remain friends?
- What are some ways people respond to conflict?
- How do you recognize and understand conflict?
- How do you resolve conflict?
- What are some forms of conflict?
- Why do some people get angry more than others when there is conflict?
- Why do some individuals always seem to be in conflict with someone else?
- What are some of the causes of conflict?
- Why do some people become violent as a result of conflict?
- What are some forms of violence?
- What are some nonviolent means to resolve conflicts?
- How can we help violent people become nonviolent?
- Are there more violent people in the United States than there are in other countries?
- If guns are often used in violence, why don't we have more gun control legislation?
- How does the justice system deal with violent people?

After the class has thought about what they want to know and the questions are formulated, it is time to organize the study. Ask the students to review all of their questions in order to develop a list of subtopics that represent the questions. Remind them that one question often relates to more than one subtopic. In the large group, guide students to generate a list. The following list of subtopics on interpersonal conflict might give you ideas as you and your students make your own list.

Subtopics on Interpersonal Conflict

- Conflict resolution between individuals
- Kinds of interpersonal conflict
- Explanation of interpersonal conflict
- Causes of interpersonal conflict
- Management of conflict
- Negotiation
- Arbitration
- Mediation
- Violence resulting from conflict
- Prevention of violence
- Justice system and violent individuals

A list of subtopics has been decided on, and now a web can be made. Web the major subtopics that you and the students have identified and then add subordinate ideas to the subtopics. You will probably web on the chalkboard or overhead and then copy the final web on paper so that students can refer to it later.

Form Study Committees

After completing a web, the students should be organized into study committees. You and the students need to decide with whom students will work in their small groups and what topics they prefer to research. If you have a group of twenty-four students, for example, you might form six groups with four students in each group. You might want to limit the number of subtopics to six, with each group studying one of the subtopics.

Develop Questions

Students must be interested enough in a topic to raise questions and explore those questions through research. Ask each group to develop as many questions as they can think of and then record them on a blank transparency so they can share them with the rest of the class and hear their comments.

If you have a study committee on "Conflict Resolution Between Individuals" (the first subtopic listed), the students might develop some of the following questions, or you might suggest that they research some of these questions.

Questions on Conflict Resolution Between Individuals

- What is conflict resolution?
- What are the different stages of conflict?
- What are different methods of resolving conflict?
- Why do we choose one method over another?
- Who is involved in conflict resolution?
- What are the benefits of conflict resolution?
- What happens in conflict resolution?
- What is the difference between resolution and settlement?

Study Topic

Once students have identified questions relevant to their topic, they begin their study. As students engage in study, they add questions and delete some of the original ones. They use many resources, including books, nonprint sources, magazines, newspapers, and computers.

Fiction Trade Books

The Cay by Theodore Taylor. New York: Doubleday, 1987. [MS] Phillip is horrified to find himself blind and stranded on an unknown island with an aged Black man. The two begin an amazing adventure that allows Phillip to really "see" for the first time.

Charlie Pippin by Candy Dawson Boyd. New York: Macmillan, 1987. [I/MS] Chartreuse "Charlie" Pippin is a smart, spunky sixth grader who just can't seem to get along with her father. He doesn't agree with her entrepreneurial skills and he absolutely refuses to discuss the Vietnam War or to help with her school project on the subject. Determined Charlie finally finds the catalyst for a reconciliation with her father.

The Cybil War by Betsy Byars. New York: Puffin, 1990. [I] Simon learns what friendship is and is not when he and his long-time best friend, Tony, get a crush on the same girl. Simon finally learns to assert himself when Tony's manipulative ways become too much.

A Dog on Barkham Street by Mary Stolz. New York: HarperCollins, 1985. [I] Edward is sick of being bullied by Martin Hastings, and he desperately wants a dog of his own. With the help of his Uncle Josh and Josh's collie Argess, Edward's life begins to change.

The Golden Goblet by Eloise Jarvis McGraw. New York: Puffin, 1986. [MS] Ranofer, a young boy in ancient Egypt, struggles against the abuse of his half-brother, Gebu. When Ranofer accidently discovers a golden goblet among Gebu's things, he realizes his brother is involved in hideous crimes. He devises a plan to help capture his brother and, as a result, his own life is reshaped.

Shiloh by Phyllis Reynolds Naylor. New York: Antheneum, 1991. [I] Marty rescues a dog that has been mistreated by its owner and the law says the dog has to be returned to its abuser. Readers sympathize with eleven-year-old Marty as he stands up for principles he knows are right.

Spider Boy by Ralph Fletcher. New York: Clarion, 1997. [MS] Bobby Ballenger, a seventh grader who loves spiders, has just moved with his family from Illinois to New Paltz, New York. In his new school he gets picked on by Chick Hall, a local bully. Full of delicious, gruesome facts about spiders, this book is about the survival instincts of a two-legged species—the new kid in school.

The War With Grandpa by Robert Kimmel Smith. New York: Dell, 1995. [MS] Peter is thrilled to learn that his grandpa is coming to live at his house. That is, until his grandpa moves into his bedroom. Peter and his friends make intricate plans to force grandpa out, but grandpa is wise to their plans and makes his own.

Wonder by Rachel Vail. New York: Puffin, 1993. [MS] Life for twelve-year-old Jessica changes for the worse when she enters junior high and finds herself dumped by her lifelong best friend. Not only does she lose her best friend, she finds herself a complete social outcast and stuck with the nickname "Wonder."

Nonfiction Trade Books

Crime in America by Milton Meltzer. New York: Morrow, 1990. [MS] Meltzer presents a comprehensive overview with facts and explanations of crime in America. He addresses both street and white-collar crime.

Peace on the Playground: Nonviolent Ways of Problem-Solving by Eileen Lucas. New York: Watts, 1991. [I] Explores the value of peaceful resolutions of problems. Includes brief biographical sketches of people such as Gandhi and King who advocated nonviolence, and suggests ways children can become peacemakers.

When Kids Drive Kids Crazy: How to Get Along with Your Friends and Enemies by Eda LeShan. New York: Dial, 1990. [MS] In this book, LeShan focuses on the relationships between adolescents. She explains why children are often cruel to each other, discusses how to deal with unkindness, and how to make friendships work.

Your Circle of Friends by Claudine G. Wirths. New York: Twenty-First Century Books, 1993. [I] A "self-help" book in the Time to Be a Teen series. It discusses in dialogue format how to make, keep, help, and lose friends.

Express Knowledge

class 1. Choose a favorite cartoon character and draw cartoons using your character illustrating the right and wrong way to solve conflicts with others.

class 2. Choose a conflict that could actually happen, such as someone pushing in line ahead of you. List the different choices you could make to resolve the situation.

3. Analyze how you resolve conflicts in your life. Include how you interact with family, friends, classmates, and teachers. List some of the choices you make that help achieve resolution.

H.W. 4. Collect newspaper clippings of stories that report on conflict in your community, state, nation, and the world. Categorize the stories and display them on a bulletin board or poster.

5. Identify a real or imaginary interpersonal conflict in your life. Make a list of all the possible ways to solve the problem without violence. When you have completed the list, evaluate the proposed solutions and compare your results with those of a peer.

6. Listen to a city council meeting or a public debate on a local public television or radio station. Make a list of the issues on which there is disagreement, and identify the possible causes of the conflict and possible ways to resolve some problems.

7. Make a list of different interpersonal conflicts that occur in different settings, such as home, school, and community. Is the conflict caused by poor communication, different interests, conflicting roles, disagreement about rules, a history of conflicts, or other reasons? Analyze the list in terms of which conflicts can or cannot be avoided, and whether the conflicts generally result in positive or negative feelings.

8. Create a list of book characters with a short summary of the characters' conflicts and their resolutions. Ask class members to discuss conflicts and resolutions from their favorite chapter books.

9. Conduct a poll of students and teachers or of family and community members on one issue related to conflict, such as gun control, the length of prison terms, or crime prevention. Present your results in graphic form.

10. Make a list of the most common conflict situations encountered by students your age. Develop short skits in which you and others role-play the conflict with scenes that show different ways to resolve the conflict. Perform the skits for your class and other classes.

11. Create a resource file of people who offer conflict resolution training, places where a person can go to learn the process, and the

processes that are taught. Begin by asking the school counselor and principal for suggestions. Make telephone calls to law enforcement and mental health agencies for their input. Share your results with others and offer a copy of your file to the school counselor and principal.

12. Collect pictures from newspapers and magazines that show people engaged in conflict situations. Classify the pictures according to the type of conflict (personal, cultural, local, state, national, and international).

13. Keep a personal journal for a period of several days. Document every situation in which you either encounter or observe conflict. Make notes about any negotiation you observed between or among the people and compromises that were reached. Compare your journals with those of other class members.

Select Topic: Intergroup Conflict

Conflict between groups can contribute to the improvement of the groups and to the larger group as well. However, as is true with interpersonal conflict, violence might occur if the groups do not appropriately engage in conflict. Dr. Martin Luther King, Jr., understood how to manage intergroup conflict in appropriate and nonviolent ways in order to bring about an improvement in society for all.

Make Lists and Web

What We Want to Know

- What is intergroup conflict?
- What are some causes of this conflict?
- How is this conflict resolved or settled?
- What are the benefits of intergroup conflict?
- How has conflict between groups about equal rights for minorities in the United States improved life for everyone?
- How has conflict between groups about equal rights for women in the United States improved life for everyone?
- How has nonviolent action worked during conflict?
- Who have been the major leaders in the conflict over civil rights for minorities and women?
- What are some of the major U.S. legislative decisions that improved civil rights for all?

Subtopics on Intergroup Conflict

- Nonviolent action in intergroup conflict
- Causes of conflict
- Conflict resolution
- Leaders in civil rights
- Outcomes of intergroup conflict
- Major legislative decisions involving civil rights of minorities
- Major legislative decisions involving civil rights of women

Form Study Committees and Develop Questions

Questions on Nonviolent Action in Intergroup Conflict

- What are the major premises of nonviolent action?
- H.W. • Who have been major leaders in the United States who have advocated nonviolent action? *What did they do?*
- H.W. • Who was Mahatma Gandhi and how did he influence Dr. Martin Luther King, Jr.?
- What are the characteristics of Dr. Martin Luther King, Jr., that made him successful with nonviolent action?
- How does nonviolent action relate to conflict resolution?
- What are some examples of nonviolent action?
- What are some major documents that demonstrate nonviolent action?

Study Topic

Fiction Trade Books

The Middle of Somewhere: A Story of South Africa by Sheila Gordon. New York: Orchard Books, 1990. [I] Whites plan to relocate Black residents and develop the village where Rebecca, age nine, and her best friend Noni have spent their childhood playing together. Apartheid, both subtle and blatant, is revealed from a young girl's perspective in this family story set in South Africa.

? *Waiting for the Rain* by Sheila Gordon. New York: Orchard Books, 1987. [MS] Two boys, one Black, one White, have been friends since early childhood. Gordon provides insights into a particular period of history in South Africa.

Nonfiction Trade Books

The Chinese-American Heritage by David M. Brownstone. New York: Facts on File, 1988. [I/MS] This book begins with a brief history of China and the events that led to the immigration of many Chinese starting in the middle of the nineteenth century. The author explains the prejudicial myths about the immigrants and the close family and ethnic ties they developed to overcome the difficulties they faced.

Freedom's Children: Young Civil Rights Activists Tell Their Own Stories by Ellen Levine. New York: Putnam, 1993. [MS] Thirty African Americans who were children and teenagers during the 1950s and 1960s tell stories of their experiences during the civil rights movement. Black-and-white photographs and brief biographies of the presenters are included.

Hate Groups by Sharon Elaine Thompson. San Diego: Lucent, 1994. [I/MS] Examines hate groups in the United States by citing examples of hate crimes and associated violence resulting from prejudice concerning race, religion, ethnic background, and sexual orientation. The author's solution to the problem involves learning how to accept and appreciate the differences of others.

Illegal Immigrants by Kathleen Lee. San Diego: Lucent, 1996. [I/MS] Addresses illegal and legal immigration in the United States. The challenge of both economic migrants and political refugees is discussed.

It's Our World, Too! Stories of Young People Who Are Making a Difference by Phillip Hoose. Boston: Joy Street, 1993. [I/MS] This important book will convince readers that they, too, can become activists and make a difference, and Hoose includes specific instructions on how to begin. The book features true stories of children and youths who have been socially active.

The March on Washington by James Haskins. New York: HarperCollins, 1993. [I/MS] This excellent book provides an in-depth study of the 1963 March on Washington. Haskins tells of events that led to the march and provides interesting details about the logistics.

Mississippi Challenge by Mildred Pitts Walter. New York: Bradbury Press, 1992. [MS] Walter recounts the brutal history of race relations in Mississippi and of the efforts of African Americans to obtain the rights of citizenship. She tells about the founding of the Mississippi Freedom Democratic Party, and about Fannie Lou Hamer and others who worked so courageously on behalf of civil rights.

Mohandas Gandhi: The Power of the Spirit by Victoria Sherrow. Brookfield, CT: Millbrook, 1994. [MS] Sherrow draws heavily on Gandhi's autobiography and other documented sources to tell the story of a man whose policy of nonviolence changed the world. She begins with his personal experience of racism in South Africa and follows his lifetime fight against oppression, first in South Africa and then in his native India.

Murder on the Highway: The Viola Liuzzo Story by Beatrice Siegal. Washington, DC: Four Winds, 1994. [MS] A foreword by Rosa Parks introduces this account of the 1965 march from Selma to Montgomery, Alabama. The book centers on the role and murder of Viola Liuzzo, a White woman from Detroit who came to support the struggle for civil rights, but it is also a history of the movement.

Nelson Mandela: Voice of Freedom by Libby Hughes. New York: Dillon, 1992. [I] In this book in the People in Focus series, Hughes describes the life of Mandela, and the struggle of different races in South Africa and other parts of the world to end apartheid. The author also covers intertribal conflicts.

Pushing the Limits: American Women, 1940–1961 by Elaine Tyler May. New York: Oxford University Press, 1994. [MS] The author uses primary sources as she describes the changing roles of women from 1940 to 1961 and takes the reader from Rosie the Riveter in World War I to Betty Friedan. She discusses social issues and includes women from different ethnic groups.

Still a Nation of Immigrants by Brent Ashabranner, photographs by Jennifer Ashabranner. New York: Cobblehill, 1993. [MS] This book deals with a number of issues related to immigration: policies, trends in migrating populations, maintaining ethnic identity, and others. The photographs introduce immigrants from a variety of countries.

Tinker vs. Des Moines: Student Rights on Trial by Doreen Rappaport. New York: HarperCollins, 1993. [I/MS] A well-researched book in the Be the Judge/Be the Jury series. The reader reviews the actual testimony and briefs and decides the outcome of this landmark case in which three students in Iowa sued school officials for suspending them for wearing black arm bands in protest of the Vietnam War.

War in Yugoslavia: The Breakup of a Nation by Edward R. Ricciuti. Highland Park, NJ: Millbrook, 1993. [I] This book clearly describes the ancient rivalry that led to the splintering of Yugoslavia. Using photographs and maps, the author explains the new republics and their status as of November 1992.

Who Cares?: Millions Do . . . A Book about Altruism by Milton Meltzer. New York: Walker, 1994. [I/MS] Meltzer demonstrates how individuals and philanthropic organizations have made a difference in our world, from the establishment of the Underground Railroad to current work against social injustice.

Witnesses to Freedom: Young People Who Fought for Civil Rights by Belinda Rochelle. New York: Lodestar, 1993. [I] Profiles eight young African Americans who risked their lives for the civil rights movement in the

1950s and 1960s. Includes direct quotations from the young people and events such as the Montgomery, Alabama, bus boycott, the sit-in movement, and the freedom rides.

Youth in the Middle East: Voices of Despair by David J. Abodaher. New York: Watts, 1990. [MS] Abodaher clearly describes the history of violence in Egypt, Israel, and Lebanon, and its impact on young people. The book leads up to the period just before the Persian Gulf War.

Zlata's Diary: A Child's Life in Sarajevo by Zlata Filipovic. New York: Viking, 1994. [I/MS] Thirteen-year-old Zlata tells about the war in Sarajevo. She records changes in her life and neighborhood.

Express Knowledge

1. Conduct a survey in your class or school on a civil rights topic. Make a report of your findings.

2. Make a collage that depicts progress toward equality made by a minority group or by women.

3. Write a short biography of Dr. Martin Luther King, Jr., or another civil rights leader citing how he/she advocated conflict resolution through nonviolent means.

4. Read the Bill of Rights from the United States Constitution. Make a list of laws or rules in your school and community that are guaranteed by the Bill of Rights.

5. Imagine that you are a member of a minority group who lives in a nondemocratic country. Make a list of the freedoms that minority groups are entitled to have in the United States that may not be guaranteed in a nondemocratic country.

6. Collect newspaper clippings that tell about individuals or members of groups of people who believe their civil rights have been violated. Display and label each clipping with the number of the Bill of Rights amendment that is alleged to be violated.

7. Dramatize negative situations that members of minority groups have endured throughout the history of the United States (an example would be the situation that confronted Rosa Parks). Perform your dramatization for class members.

8. Trace the history of women's rights for Native Americans and immigrant women. Make a chart describing progress that has been made and improvements still to be made. Consider illustrating then-and-now situations.

9. Divide the countries of the world into three groups: democracies with few civil rights violations, democracies with reported civil rights violations, and nondemocratic countries with some civil

rights violations. Compile your results and consider creating a world map using color to depict the three groups.

10. Study one ethnic or cultural group of people who are still oppressed. Prepare a written or oral report about the group, including recommendations for ways to remedy the situation.

11. Write a constitution for your school with a bill of rights.

Select Topic: Military Conflict

Students are naturally interested in the nature of military conflict. Before students finish middle school, most have studied the fall of the Roman Empire, the Crusades, Indian wars, the American Revolutionary War, the Civil War, the War of 1812, World Wars I and II, and other military actions. Students are especially interested in peaceful resolutions for military conflicts; they enjoy studying peacekeeping organizations such as the United Nations. Themes on military conflict help students realize the need for a safe and more humane world. This theme encompasses military conflict in general. The other themes on military action are specific to several different wars.

Make Lists and Web

What We Want to Know

- Who starts war?
- What are the causes of war?
- What are the objectives of war?
- How are the troops drafted?
- How are a country's resources used for war?
- How much money do wars cost?
- How is money diverted from health and education programs to war efforts?
- How are natural resources such as water, grasslands, forests, fossil fuels, and minerals depleted because of war?
- Why are religious conflicts a source for war?
- What wars have been fought over territorial issues?
- What weapons are used in conflict?
- Where does the fighting occur?
- What are events that lead up to a war?
- How is propaganda used in a war?
- What are events that end a war?

- What are examples of total war and limited war?
- What are differences and similarities between wars?
- How is the United Nations involved in wars?
- What was the public's response to particular wars?

Subtopics on Military Conflict

- Objectives of war
- Cost of war
- Territorial aggression
- Economic burden
- Major battles
- Environmental concerns
- Causes
- Compromises
- Leaders
- Treaties
- Refugees
- Human rights violations during war
- Suffering
- Speeches
- Outcomes
- Public response to war
- Major wars
- Weapons (conventional, nuclear, chemical, biological)
- Weapons race
- Terrorism
- Colonialism
- Democracy concerns
- United Nations involvement

Form Study Committees and Develop Questions

Questions on the Cost of War

- What are the military costs around the globe each year and in past years for the different wars?
- How much is spent on the world's militaries?
- How much of the gross national product of a country is spent on the military?

- How are many of the best minds of a country used for war (military research, leadership, scientists, engineers)?
- Why is the weapons industry the world's second largest industry after oil?
- Why is much of the computer science research in the world being conducted to increase defense capabilities?
- How many people are employed as soldiers or as workers in the military industry?
- What global problems could be solved if money weren't spent on the military and war?
- How much money is diverted to war from health and social programs?
- How are natural resources such as grasslands, forests, fossil fuels, or minerals depleted because of war?

Study Topic

Fiction and nonfiction trade books about different wars in United States history are included in theme immersions for the Revolutionary War, War of 1812, Civil War, Spanish-American War, World War I, World War II, and recent military conflicts including Vietnam, Korea, and the Persian Gulf War. Therefore, we have listed no books for this section, but refer you to the other sections on specific military conflicts.

Express Knowledge

1. Select a war and develop a list of heroes and heroines of the war. By each name, give a brief explanation of why they were strong individuals, why they were famous, what they gave up for the war, and their most heroic action.

2. Draw a map of the world. Mark all the countries that currently have conflicts or wars.

3. Choose a war and make a chart of the cost of war for the different countries involved. Discuss how the money could have been spent to improve the quality of life for the citizens of the countries.

4. Write a musical satire to the tune of the song, "We Will All Go Together When We Go," or "So Long, It's Been Good to Know You."

5. Pretend you are a soldier in a particular war and write a letter home about where you are, the conditions, the weapons you use, the things you miss from home, and the feelings you have.

6. Develop a television documentary about the events and personal sacrifices of the military and civilians in war.

7. Draw a picture of a battle scene before and after the conflict.

8. Draw pictures of different military uniforms and weapons.

9. Write an obituary for a famous war personality. List the greatest achievements and/or most significant events in his/her life.

10. Draw a map of the part of the world where a conflict has occurred. Track the movement of troops, battle sites, command posts, etc.

11. Prepare a television newscast about a battle or war. Act as a television reporter who is reporting from the country where the conflict occurs. Discuss the conflict, the living conditions, the feelings of the civilians, the amount of damage, etc.

12. Create a timeline of a war by researching history. Attach a long piece of butcher paper to one wall of the classroom or hall. Draw a line across the paper and divide it into one-year increments. Place the significant battles and events of the war on the timeline and illustrate.

13. Follow one current conflict in the world for one week or more. Read newspapers and magazines and make notes about the different issues, the conflicting attitudes, the spending, military and civilian losses, etc. Make a bulletin board or scrapbook of clippings of articles, editorials, and photographs. Write your own opinion piece to display with your clippings.

14. Write an editorial for the school or city newspaper explaining your views on a current military conflict.

15. Create a chart giving the number of people who died in various wars.

16. Make a chart listing the causes of different wars. Include possible solutions and list any compromises and treaties.

17. Many women and members of minority groups have been marginalized because of historical interpretations of particular wars. Develop a speech or write an essay on why you believe these errors in history have occurred.

18. Find two newspaper or magazine articles or editorials that present contradictory information about a current conflict in the world. List the differences between the points of view, why you think the authors are in conflict, and the sources of their information.

19. Check the *Readers' Guide to Periodical Literature* or do a computer search to see how many articles or books have been written about a particular war. Make inferences about the number and selected titles. Summarize your thinking in a written or oral report.

20. Plan and perform a mock summit between or among different leaders related to a crisis situation.

21. Research the drafting of soldiers for the Civil War and other wars during American history. Find out if it was possible to earn an exemption to the draft or to pay the government to be excluded from the draft. Present your findings in an oral or written report.

22. Publish a historical newspaper that is representative of the particular historical time around one war in the history of the United States.

Select Topic: Revolutionary War

The colonists were angered by the extreme tax laws imposed by Great Britain, such as the Sugar Act in 1764 and the Stamp Act in 1765. In response to the Tea Act, passed by the British Parliament in 1773, some colonists, led by Samuel Adams, protested by dressing as Indians and throwing chests of tea into Boston Harbor on December 16, 1773.

With this act of resistance and subsequent counteractions by the British, the colonists began to unite against British rule, with many believing that they should gain independence from Great Britain. When the First Continental Congress met in Philadelphia in September 1774, they decided to ask the king of England for repeal of the taxation acts. They received no answer.

On April 18, 1775, the first battle of the war between the colonists and the British occurred at Lexington and then Concord. After this battle, the Second Continental Congress met in May 1775 and asked George Washington to take command of the colonial forces in Boston.

In June 1776 the Second Continental Congress decided to take action and write a paper declaring the colonies' independence from Great Britain. On July 4, 1776, the Continental Congress adopted the Declaration of Independence.

Once the colonists declared their independence, they had to fight the British in order to gain it. The Revolutionary War was fought between 1776 and 1781. The colonists won the war for a number of reasons. General George Washington, the commander of the armed forces, was a talented and effective military leader. Benjamin Franklin, an American representative in France, encouraged the French to join the American cause. The distance the British had to travel with troops and provisions also proved to be a major obstacle.

The British surrendered at Yorktown in 1781, ending the war. However, the formal peace treaty, the Treaty of Paris, was not signed by the British and the Americans until 1783. As a result of the treaty, the United States became an independent nation.

Make Lists and Web

What We Want to Know

- Who were major leaders in the colonies?
- Why did France help the colonists?
- What were the political and social beliefs of the colonists?
- What weapons were used in the war?
- Why did England want to maintain control over the colonies?
- Why did some colonists remain loyal to the mother country?
- How strong was the Continental Army?
- Why did the colonists have such a strong desire for self-government?
- What were major contributions of Thomas Jefferson?
- What effect did the independence of the colonists have on other parts of the world?
- What were the Sugar Act, the Townshend Act, and the Intolerable Acts?
- How did the colonists respond when England insisted that colonists house the British soldiers?
- How was the Continental Army organized?
- What were the major battles of the war?
- How did the colonists win their independence?

Subtopics on the Revolutionary War

- Declaration of Independence
- Involvement of other countries
- English land ownership laws
- Stamp, Sugar, Townshend, and Intolerable acts
- Major battles
- Weapons
- Leaders
- Demands by Britain that incensed the colonists
- Reasons the colonists won the war

Form Study Committees and Develop Questions

Questions on the Declaration of Independence

- Why was the Declaration written?
- Who was the author of the Declaration and how did that person go about writing it?

- What are the major points in the document?
- Who were the signers of the document and what were their backgrounds?
- Where was it signed and what were the circumstances surrounding the formal signing?
- What impact did the Declaration of Independence have on the colonists and on England?

Study Topic

Fiction Trade Books

Finishing Becca: A Story About Peggy Shippen and Benedict Arnold by Ann Rinaldi. San Diego: Harcourt Brace, 1994. [MS] As Peggy Shippen's young maid, Becca witnesses Peggy's marriage to Benedict Arnold and how she influenced Arnold to betray the Patriot forces. In this historical novel, Becca seeks to find her "missing pieces" and to define her loyalties.

Guns for General Washington: A Story of the American Revolution by Seymour Reit. San Diego: Harcourt Brace, 1990. [I] Tells the story of how young Will Knox and his brother, Henry, undertake the almost impossible task of transporting 183 cannons in midwinter from Fort Ticonderoga to Boston. Their heroic action helps George Washington win an important battle early in the American Revolution.

The Riddle of Pencroft Farm by Dorothea Jensen. San Diego: Harcourt/Gulliver, 1989. [I] Twelve-year-old Lars Olafson is not happy when his parents move to rural Pennsylvania to live with an elderly aunt on Pencroft Farm. He becomes happier, though, when he meets the elusive Geordie and begins to hear two-hundred-year-old stories of Valley Forge and George Washington and when Geordie helps him solve the mystery of his aunt's missing will.

A Ride into Morning: The Story of Tempe Wick by Ann Rinaldi. San Diego: Harcourt Brace, 1991. [MS] This historical novel, a book in the Great Episodes series, is based on a real event that took place during the American Revolution. Tempe Wick is worried about caring for her sick mother and maintaining the farm when a soldier commands her to loan him her beloved horse in exchange for keeping her brother's secret from the authorities.

1787 by Joan Anderson, illustrated by Alexander Farquharson. San Diego: Harcourt Brace, 1987. [I/MS] Young Jared Mifflin is selected to serve as James Madison's aide for the Constitutional Convention during the summer of 1787. A blending of fact and fiction introduces the reader to this fateful summer and to both real and fictional participants in the convention.

Nonfiction Trade Books

Abigail Adams: Witness to a Revolution by Natalie S. Bober. New York: Atheneum, 1995. [I/MS] Bober interweaves excerpts from Abigail Adams's correspondence into this superbly researched biography of the wife and mother of presidents. The reader learns about Adams as well as about significant people, events, and decisions of the era.

The American Revolution: How We Fought the War of Independence by Edward F. Dolan. Highland Park, NJ: Millbrook, 1995. [I/MS] Dolan outlines the American Revolution from Lexington to Yorktown, including people, events, and battles. This well-researched book has numerous illustrations—maps, sketches, reproductions, and paintings.

The American Revolution: War for Independence by Alden Carter. New York: Watts, 1992. [I] Part of the First Books series and a good introduction to the Revolution. Carter traces the origin of the conflict with England, gives comprehensive summaries of the events and battles, and adds some human elements to the subject.

The American Revolutionaries: A History in Their Own Words by Milton Meltzer. New York: Crowell, 1987. [I/MS] Prints, photographs, and primary source materials are used to capture the meaning of the American Revolution (for those who lived through it). Meltzer introduces the sources with brief explanations.

The Battle of Lexington and Concord by Neil Johnson. Old Tappan, NJ: Four Winds, 1992. [I] Recounts the famous battle between the Minutemen and the British Redcoats. Photographs taken at full-dress reenactments on Patriots Day bring the event to life.

Becoming American: Young People in the American Revolution by P. M. Zall. New Haven, CT: Linnet, 1993. [MS] The author uses excerpts from teenagers' letters and journals to describe aspects of life during and following the Revolutionary War. War, work, politics, and family life are discussed.

Founding Mothers: Women in America in the Revolutionary Era by Linda Grant DePauw. Boston: Houghton Mifflin, 1975. [I/MS] This excellent book describes the daily lives, social roles, and contributions of women of different ethnic groups and social classes who lived during the Revolutionary era. DePauw quotes from primary sources and uncovers some unusual facts as she tells stories of women soldiers, spies, organizers, couriers, and political activists.

George Washington: Leader of a New Nation by Mary Pope Osborne. New York: Dial, 1991. [I] This is an interesting and well-documented biography. Osborne uses diary entries, letters, texts of speeches, thoughts of people who knew him, and a timeline of his life to show both the public and private Washington.

The Memoirs of Andrew Sherburne, Patriot and Privateer of the American Revolution by Karen Zeinert (editor), illustrated by Seymour Fleishman. New Haven, CT: Linnet, 1993. [MS] Andrew Sherburne, a privateer in the colonial navy at age thirteen, set out to sea to plunder British ships. Seymour adapted Sherburne's 1828 autobiography and includes historical notes.

Revolutionary War: A Sourcebook on Colonial America by Carter Smith (editor). Brookfield, CT: Millbrook, 1991. [MS] This book is in the American Albums from the Collection of the Library of Congress series. It contains brief text and reproductions of documents from the Library of Congress.

Songs and Stories from the American Revolution by Jerry Silverman. Brookfield, CT: Millbrook, 1994. [I] History and period musical techniques are included in this introduction to the American Revolution. Ten songs are presented with full scores for piano, guitar, and voice.

Thomas Jefferson: The Revolutionary Aristocrat by Milton Meltzer. New York: Watts, 1991. [MS] Meltzer examines Jefferson's successes and failures, both personal and political, in this well-researched and interesting biography. The book is illustrated with portraits, maps, and documents from the period.

The War for Independence: the Story of the American Revolution by Albert Marrin. New York: Atheneum, 1988. [I/MS] Marrin's chapter on the "secret war" of spies and codes will be especially attractive to younger readers of this fine overview of the war. The author has woven hundreds of facts into this account of the war and its key figures.

A Young Patriot: The American Revolution as Experienced by One Boy by Jim Murphy. New York: Clarion Books, 1996. [I/MS] Teenager Joseph Plumb Martin speaks for himself in this excellent book on the Revolutionary War. Martin fought under Washington, Lafayette, and Steuben, and took part in major battles.

Express Knowledge

1. Imagine that you are a member of a colonial family and you are required to house a British soldier. Write a letter to a friend telling how you feel about this situation.
2. Make a speech to other colonists about one of the following acts that were especially disliked by the colonists: Sugar, Stamp, Townshend, and Intolerable.
3. Write an obituary for a Revolutionary War leader.
4. Decide to be a loyalist or a supporter of the Continental Congress. Write a position paper that states the reasons for your decision.
5. Write a report about the contributions of African Americans to the Revolutionary War.

6. Copy some of your favorite phrases from the Declaration of Independence and write your ideas about them, including why they are your favorite phrases.

7. Make diagrams showing the different weapons used during the Revolutionary War.

8. Read Henry Wadsworth Longfellow's poem "Paul Revere's Ride." Adapt it to a choral reading for a small group or for the entire class to read.

9. Hypothesize what would have happened if England had won the Revolutionary War. Write what you imagine might have happened and when and if independence might have occurred.

10. Criticize the manner in which England treated the colonies. Make a list of your criticisms.

11. Draw a timeline that shows the events, including battles, that occurred between 1775 and 1783.

Select Topic: War of 1812

Americans became angered again when British ships stopped American ships and captured some sailors. The Americans were further angered when in 1809, the British were supporting the actions of Indians against Americans. In 1812, Congress declared war against Britain.

In August 1814, the British invaded Washington, D.C., and burned much of the city. A month later they attacked Fort McHenry in Baltimore. As a young American lawyer, Francis Scott Key, watched the flag still flying in the battle, he realized how much the flag and his country meant to him and wrote the poem "The Star-Spangled Banner," which was set to music later and became our national anthem.

A peace treaty was signed in December 1814. However, because of the slow communications of the day, many people did not know about the peace treaty for some time. Thus, in January 1815 the British army attacked New Orleans. The British suffered many casualties and the Americans suffered few. Andrew Jackson, the military leader and hero of the Battle of New Orleans, gained fame from the battle, and later became president of the United States.

Make Lists and Web

What We Want to Know

- How were Britain and France involved in the War of 1812?
- Why did Britain stop ships of the United States and how did the United States respond?
- Who was the president at the time of the war?

- What was the 1807 incident on Chesapeake Bay and why was it important?
- Why was the 1807 Embargo Act disastrous to the economy of New England?
- Why was trade a problem between the United States, England, and France?
- What are the reasons why the War of 1812 would not have been fought if today's technology had been available?
- What effect would today's technology have on the Battle of New Orleans?
- Why were U.S. citizens so angry with England?
- Why did the War Hawks and the Federalists disagree on going to war?
- Was the United States prepared to fight the British?
- What inspired Francis Scott Key to write the words to "The Star-Spangled Banner"?
- Why was the Battle of New Orleans unnecessary?
- Who were the major military leaders in the war?
- What were the main points of the Treaty of Ghent?

Subtopics on the War of 1812
- "The Star-Spangled Banner"
- War between France and England
- War Hawks and Federalists
- Leaders, including James Madison and Andrew Jackson
- Battle of Tippecanoe
- Trade factors, including the embargoes
- Battle of New Orleans
- Treaty of Ghent

Form Study Committees and Develop Questions

Questions on "The Star-Spangled Banner"
- Who composed "The Star-Spangled Banner?"
- Under what conditions was it written?
- What was the original name of the poem?
- What was the profession of the composer?
- Who composed the music for the poem? Why?

- When and how did "The Star-Spangled Banner" become the national anthem?
- What controversy surrounds the song?

Study Topic

Nonfiction Trade Books

By the Dawn's Early Light: The Story of "The Star-Spangled Banner" by Steven Kroll, illustrated by Dan Andreasen. New York: Scholastic, 1994. [I] Contains some background information about the War of 1812 and Key's involvement in the war. A reproduction of the original manuscript of the anthem is included.

1812: The War Nobody Won by Albert Marrin. New York: Atheneum, 1985. [I/MS] Diagrams, old maps, and prints illustrate the War of 1812. Events such as Dolley Madison's escape from the White House and Key's writing of "The Star-Spangled Banner" are included.

The Great Little Madison by Jean Fritz. New York: Putnam, 1991. [I] Prints and engravings enhance this interesting, humorous biography of our fourth president. Fritz includes Madison's attendance at the Continental Congress and the Constitutional Convention.

The War of 1812 by Peter I. Bosco. Brookfield, CT: Millbrook, 1991. [I] Bosco recounts the early days of the United States and the problems that led to the War of 1812. He gives the causes and effects of the war and reports on the sea battles of our fledgling navy.

The War of 1812 by Richard B. Morris. Minneapolis: Lerner, 1985. A volume in the American History Topic Books series. Morris discusses the causes, major events, and results of the War of 1812.

Express Knowledge

1. Write a brief biography of President James Madison.
2. Draw a map of the United States at the time of the War of 1812. On the map, show the major U.S. and British offensives of the war.
3. Write a brief history of "The Star-Spangled Banner."
4. Reenact the Battle of New Orleans in the classroom.
5. Analyze the events of the War of 1812 to determine why both Britain and the United States claimed to have won. Write the results of your analysis.
6. Summarize the battles of the War of 1812. Include the dates, the locations, the generals, the number of troops, events leading to battle, and the outcomes.

7. Study the events leading to the war and then write your prediction of what would have happened if the communication systems available today had been available to world leaders in 1812.

8. Pretend you are representing the United States in Ghent, Belgium, and a classmate is representing the British government. Write notes for your negotiations and then role-play the meeting leading to the Treaty of Ghent.

9. Explain how Napoléon was indirectly involved in the War of 1812. Develop a monologue that Napoléon might have uttered telling why he should not be blamed for the war.

10. Write a biography of Dolley Madison and highlight her life in the White House and her role in saving items during the War of 1812 that are today of historical interest.

Select Topic: Civil War

The Civil War, the war between the North and the South, lasted from 1861 to 1865. The South (Confederacy) fought for Southern independence. The North wanted to maintain the Union and keep the Southern states from seceding.

Abraham Lincoln was president of the United States during the war. Lincoln called for war in order to preserve the Union, not to end slavery. However, in January 1863, he issued the Emancipation Proclamation. This document made it clear that slavery would end if the North won the war.

The first battle of the war occurred at Bull Run, a small creek between Washington, D.C., and Richmond, Virginia. When the Union Army was defeated, it was realized that the war would be a long one. As the war progressed, however, the South steadily lost ground. On April 9, 1865, General Robert E. Lee of the Confederate Army surrendered to General Ulysses S. Grant of the Union Army at Appomattox, Virginia. The war was over; unfortunately, over sixty thousand people had died, and four hundred thousand had been wounded.

Make Lists and Web

What We Want to Know

- What were the causes of the Civil War?
- Who were the major leaders in the South and the North during the war?
- What were the effects on the economy?
- What major decisions were made during the war?

- What was the Underground Railroad?
- What was the role of African Americans during the war?
- How and when did the South surrender to the North?
- Why did the South surrender?
- What were some of the reasons why the South wanted to keep slavery?
- What happened to the wounded and to people with diseases?
- What were some major differences between the North and South?
- What happened after the war?
- What effect did Abraham Lincoln's assassination have on the North and the South?

Subtopics on the Civil War

- Effects of war on the economy
- States' rights versus the federal government
- Major leaders
- Slavery
- Kansas-Nebraska Act
- Dred Scott decision
- Major acts and decisions
- Underground Railroad
- Major battles
- Role of African Americans
- Cultural and economic differences between the North and the South
- Surrender
- Lincoln's assassination
- Hardships of civilians
- Effects of war on economy of North and South
- Prisons in North and South
- Results of war

Form Study Committees and Develop Questions

Questions on the Effects of War on the Economy

- What happened to the economy in the North? South?
- What were the major industries in the North before the war? South?
- What were the major industries in the North after the war? South?

- Who were major leaders in improving the economy in the South and in the North after the war?
- What were major factors that affected the economy in the North and South?

Study Topic

Fiction Trade Books

Across Five Aprils by Irene Hunt. Parsippany, NJ: Silver Burdett, 1984. [I/MS] The Creighton family lives on a farm in Illinois and becomes involved in the Civil War in April 1861. The family becomes divided by the conflicts of the war and a young boy watches as his family and community are changed during the five years of the war.

Bull Run by Paul Fleischman. New York: HarperCollins, 1993. [I/MS] Sixteen different people narrate the 1861 Battle of Bull Run, the first battle of the Civil War, and both Southern and Northern points of view are presented. The book is arranged to be used as readers' theater.

Charley Skedaddle by Patricia Beatty. New York: Morrow, 1987. [I/MS] To avenge his older brother's death at Gettysburg, twelve-year-old Charlie enlists as a drummer boy in the Union Army. Sickened by battle, he runs away and finds comfort with an elderly woman in a remote Southern valley.

Pink and Say by Patricia Polacco. New York: Philomel, 1994. [I] This moving story was passed down through generations of the author's family. Two young Union soldiers, one African American, the other Caucasian, are caught up in the travesties of war.

Red Cap by Clifton G. Wisler. New York: Lodestar, 1991. [MS] Told in first person, this novel is based on the life of thirteen-year-old Ransom J. Powell, a drummer boy for the Union Army. The book vividly portrays the bitter struggles and bloody battles of the Civil War.

Turn Homeward, Hannalee by Patricia Beatty. New York: Morrow, 1984. [I/MS] Hannalee was only twelve when she was sent north to work in a Yankee mill. This book shows the effects of the Civil War on working-class Southerners who did not own slaves.

With Every Drop of Blood by James Lincoln Collier and Christopher Collier. New York: Delacorte, 1994. [I] Fourteen-year-old Johnny had promised his Pa that he would not join the fighting, but he could not resist when offered money to transport food to the Confederate troops. After he is captured by a young African American Union soldier, an uneasy friendship develops between the two.

Nonfiction Trade Books

Behind the Blue and Gray: The Soldier's Life in the Civil War by Delia Ray. New York: HarperCollins, 1991. [MS] This book from the Young Readers' History of the Civil War series examines the lives of common soldiers, both Union and Confederate. The soldiers' experiences are well documented.

The Boys' Wars: Confederate and Union Soldiers Talk About the Civil War by Jim Murphy. New York: Clarion, 1990. [I] Actual letters and diaries are used to examine the experiences of boys under the age of sixteen who fought in the Civil War. This is a well-researched and readable book.

Civil War!: America Becomes One Nation by James I. Robertson, Jr. New York: Knopf, 1992. [I] Provides a thorough overview of the Civil War. Robertson gives a year-by-year account of the war and the battles.

Frank Thompson: Her Civil War Story by Bryna Stevens. New York: Macmillan, 1992. [I/MS] At age fifteen Sara Emma Edmonds fled her home in Canada and, disguised as a man, served in the Union Army for two years under the name of Frank Thompson. Black-and-white photographs and reproductions illustrate this compelling story.

Frederick Douglass: In His Own Words by Milton Meltzer (editor), illustrated by Stephen Alcorn. San Diego: Harcourt Brace, 1995. [MS] Though born a slave in 1818, Douglass became one of the great leaders of American history as a spokesperson for justice. In this book, Meltzer presents the writings and speeches of Douglass in three groups: "Before the War," "The War Years," and "After the War."

From Slave to Civil War Hero: The Life and Time of Robert Smalls by Michael L. Cooper. New York: Lodestar, 1994. [I] During his seventy-six years, Smalls moves from slave to free man and on to political leader. The struggles of Reconstruction, some events of the Civil War, and the social climate during the period of slavery are woven into this story of Robert Smalls.

John Brown: One Man Against Slavery by Gwen Everett, illustrated by Jacob Lawrence. New York: Rizzoli, 1993. [I] This powerful picture book presents the story of John Brown's raid on Harper's Ferry. The story is told in first-person from the viewpoint of Brown's daughter, Annie.

Just a Few Words, Mr. Lincoln: The Story of the Gettysburg Address by Jean Fritz. New York: Putnam, 1993. [I] The writing and the presentation of the Gettysburg Address are described. A copy of the famous speech is included.

The Long Road to Gettysburg by Jim Murphy. New York: Clarion, 1992. [I] Murphy focuses on a fifteen-year-old Union soldier and an eighteen-year-old

Confederate lieutenant in this account of the events at Gettysburg. The fine writing, archival photographs, and the young soldiers from opposing sides make this an outstanding account of the famous battle.

Music in the Civil War by Stephen Currie. Cincinnati: Shoe Tree, 1992. [MS] Etchings, sheet music, and newspaper drawings provide interesting illustrations. Includes historical references to songs as well as information on musicians, composers, pipers, and drummers of the time of the Civil War.

Robert E. Lee by Nathan Aaseng. Minneapolis: Lerner, 1991. [MS] A readable biography of the Confederate Army commander Robert E. Lee. Special emphasis is given to Lee's strategies as a Civil War general.

A Separate Battle: Women and the Civil War by Ina Chang. New York: Lodestar, 1991. [I/MS] Women were soldiers and spies, nurses and teachers. This history of Civil War women includes brief biographies of Louisa May Alcott, Mary Chesnut, Angelina Grimké, Sojourner Truth, and Harriet Tubman.

Unconditional Surrender: U. S. Grant and the Civil War by Albert Marrin. New York: Atheneum, 1994. [MS] This excellent, readable biography is well researched and thoroughly documented. One learns about Grant at home and at war.

Express Knowledge

1. Make a report about the raid at Harper's Ferry and the hanging of John Brown. Sing the song "John Brown's Body."

2. Write a book report on Harriet Beecher Stowe's *Uncle Tom's Cabin*. Include why the book changed many people's minds about slavery.

3. Prepare and give speeches to deliver in Congress expressing your views on slavery and saving the nation as if you were a congressional member before the war. You might want to discuss the fight in Congress between Charles Sumner and Preston Brooks, in which Brooks beat Sumner with a stick until he nearly died.

4. Conduct a debate in the classroom as if you were living in Civil War times. One of you take the position that the Union should stay intact and the other one take the position that the Southern states should secede.

5. Make diagrams that show the weapons used during the Civil War and compare them with those of the Revolutionary War.

6. Make sketches of the uniforms worn by the North and the South. Mount them for display.

7. Draw a map of the states of the North and South on poster board or on butcher paper. Mark the major battles and the routes of the marches.

8. Write an introduction to Lincoln's speech, the Emancipation Proclamation, so that the audience can better understand the speech. With two or more people, read parts of the speech.

9. Make a Venn diagram that shows the differences and similarities between Abraham Lincoln and Jefferson Davis, and between Ulysses S. Grant and Robert E. Lee.

10. Make a list of the major strengths of the South and major strengths of the North.

11. Pretend you are a young man of draft age during the Civil War. Write a letter that tells why you should be exempt from fighting in the Civil War.

Select Topic: Spanish-American War, 1898

In 1898, Cubans began fighting Spain to gain their independence. The United States government sent the battleship *Maine* to Havana, Cuba, to protect Americans living there. While it was in Havana Harbor, an explosion ripped through the battleship, killing about 260 men on board.

Congress declared war on Spain about two months after the incident. A few days later American naval ships attacked and destroyed the Spanish fleet in Manila, the Philippines. A few days later American troops landed in Cuba, defeating the Spaniards.

As a result of the war, Spain gave the United States control of Puerto Rico, Guam, and the Philippines. Theodore Roosevelt emerged from the war as a hero. He and his "Rough Riders" fought fiercely in the battle for Santiago, Cuba. His popularity helped him become elected president of the United States in 1904.

Make Lists and Web

What We Want to Know
- What were the causes of the Spanish-American War?
- Where was the war fought?
- Who were the leaders in the war?
- What was public opinion about the war?
- Did newspapers help to form public opinion?
- What were the major battle sites of the war?
- What did the United States gain from the Spanish-American War?

- What were the terms of the peace treaty?
- Why did the United States want to control the Philippines?
- Why did the United States win the war?

Subtopics on the Spanish-American War
- Concern for Cuba
- Public opinion and the newspapers
- Military leaders including Dewey, Woods, and Roosevelt
- Major battles of the war
- Major events leading up to the war
- Weapons of war, including the battleship *Maine*
- Peace treaty that ended the war
- Panama Canal
- Impact on the future role of the United States in the world

Form Study Committees and Develop Questions

Questions on public opinion and the newspapers
- What was the public's opinion about Cuba before the Spanish-American War?
- What were major elements that contributed to the concern of the American public over Cuba?
- How did newspapers affect the public's opinion about the situation in Cuba?
- Why were the newspapers so involved in the situation in Cuba?

Study Topic

Nonfiction Trade Books

The Spanish-American War by Deborah Bachrach. San Diego: Lucent, 1991. [MS] This book is in the America's Wars series and provides an overview of the Spanish-American War. Bachrach examines the historical and political background of the war, its major battles, and the effects of America's victory.

The Spanish-American War by Michael Golay. New York: Facts on File, 1995. [MS] Chronicles the causes, major events, and important military strategies of the war. The book includes quotes from soldiers, maps, photos, and a lengthy index.

The Spanish-American War by Albert Marrin. New York: Atheneum, 1991. [MS] This book begins with the 1898 sinking of the *Maine* and follows the two strands of the war. Marrin provides an informative and well-paced account of the Spanish-American War and the subsequent Philippine insurrection.

The Spanish-American War: Imperial Ambitions by Alden R. Carter. New York: Franklin Watts, 1992. [I/MS] A book in the First Book series with maps and full-color reproductions of paintings. A few personalities are mentioned, but Carter primarily provides a chronicle of the ten-week war between the United States and Spain.

The Story of the Rough Riders by Zachary Kent. Chicago: Children's Press, 1991. [I/MS] A book in the Cornerstones of Freedom series. Kent describes how Teddy Roosevelt formed his motley regiment of Rough Riders and led them into the Battle at San Juan Hill.

The Story of the Sinking of the Battleship Maine by Zachary Kent. Chicago: Children's Press, 1988. [I/MS] This book is in the Cornerstones of Freedom series and is illustrated with photographs and engravings. Kent discusses the mysterious sinking of the *Maine* and the situation in Cuba, and tells how the United States ended up at war with Spain.

Theodore Roosevelt Takes Charge by Nancy Whitelaw. Morton Grove: Whitman, 1992. [MS] This comprehensive biography covers Theodore Roosevelt's colorful life from birth to death and includes historical details of time and events. The author includes numerous photographs, a chronology of Roosevelt's life, and a list of the books he wrote.

The United States in the Spanish-American War by Don Lawson. New York: Abelard-Schuman, 1976. [MS] In this book in the Young People's History of America's Wars series, Lawson describes the precipitating causes, the key battles, and various war heroes of the Spanish-American War. He tells how the war led to the United States's involvement in the Philippine insurrection and to the Boxer Rebellion.

Express Knowledge

1. Draw a map of the Caribbean region showing Cuba and Puerto Rico. Indicate on the map the major sea and land battles of the Spanish-American War.

2. Write several newspaper headlines that are similar to the headlines of two major newspapers at the time of the Spanish-American War: *The New York Journal* and *The World*.

3. Reenact the Battle of San Juan Hill when the Rough Riders, led by Theodore Roosevelt, assaulted the fortifications of Santiago.

4. Write a biography of Theodore Roosevelt highlighting his role in the Spanish-American War.

5. Summarize Cuban history and hypothesize what might have happened if the country had become a possession of the United States following the Spanish-American War.

6. Analyze how the Spanish-American War was the beginning of the United States's status as a powerful nation.

7. Research the explosion of the battleship *Maine*. Pretend the ship was blown up today and describe what types of scientific tools are available to determine the cause or prevention of the explosion.

8. Conduct a survey asking adults who are not historians or teachers the causes of the Spanish-American War. Chart the results of your survey.

9. Compare the situation of the United States owning Guam, the Philippines, and Puerto Rico to the thirteen original colonies belonging to England.

10. Explain why it was necessary for the United States to increase military power and build the Panama Canal following the end of the Spanish-American War.

Select Topic: World War I

When war erupted in Europe in 1914, the United States remained neutral. The Central Powers (Austria-Hungary, Germany, the Ottoman Empire, and Bulgaria) and the Allied Powers (France, Great Britain, Italy, Russia, Japan, and later, the United States) fought against one another in World War I. The Germans threatened to sink all ships sailing to or from France and England, and in May 1915 sank the ocean liner *Lusitania*. Many Americans were among the thousand or more people who died. When the United States protested, the Germans stopped attacking passenger ships. However, about two years later, they started attacking all ships once again, which caused the United States to break off relations with Germany.

The United States discovered that Germany was trying to convince Mexico to enter the war with them by promising to help return to Mexico the land that was lost to the United States in 1848. These actions infuriated the Americans; therefore, in April 1917, President Woodrow Wilson asked Congress to declare war against the Central Powers.

American troops and supplies were immediately sent to Europe to support the Allies. Over one million American soldiers fought in Europe. With the support of the Americans, the Allies were winning the war by 1918. On November 11, 1918, the war ended.

Following the war, President Wilson helped to form a League of

Nations in which countries of the world would cooperate and work for world peace. European nations accepted Wilson's plan; however, the United States Congress prevented the United States from joining.

Make Lists and Web

What We Want to Know

- What were the causes of World War I?
- How did the shooting of an Austrian prince ignite the beginning of World War I?
- Why did two opposing alliances form in Europe before the war?
- Why did Americans struggle to remain neutral in the war?
- How did Germany's U-boat aggression push America to war?
- How did the United States raise, train, and equip the military?
- What was the role of the African American soldier in the war?
- What was the role of the United States soldier in the war?
- How many people died in World War I?
- What weapons were used?
- What were the major battles?
- How did geography prevent quick victory on land and sea?
- How did the war cause a massive migration of African Americans from the South to the North and West, and what impact did that migration have on all people living in the United States?
- What impact did the war have on the immigration of Mexicans into the United States?
- How did the war change the rights of women?
- What were the terms of the peace agreement at the end of the war?

Subtopics on World War I

- Effects of the war upon African Americans, women, Mexican immigrants
- Causes of the war
- Formation of Europe's opposing alliances
- America's struggle for neutrality
- No quick victory
- Reasons for America's entry into the war
- Major battles of the war

- Weapons and equipment, including poisonous gas and machine guns
- Role of the United States in the war
- Statistics of the war
- Peace treaty and other treaties resulting from war
- Personalities of the war
- Role of League of Nations
- Reparations (payment of war debts)

Form Study Committees and Develop Questions

Questions on the Effects of the War upon African Americans, Women, and Mexican Immigrants

- How many African Americans moved to the North and West during and immediately after World War I?
- What facilitated this massive migration?
- What were some of the problems that confronted African Americans when they arrived in their new homes?
- What factors contributed to the large increase in Mexican immigration into the United States during the war?
- What happened to the Mexican immigrants once they arrived in the United States?
- What were some of the roles that changed for women?
- How did women benefit from the war?
- Were all or some of the wartime gains lost after the war?

Study Topic

Fiction Trade Books

Good-bye, Billy Radish by Gloria Skurzynski. New York: Bradbury, 1992. [I/MS] This coming-of-age novel set in a Pennsylvania steel town during World War I is about the growing and changing friendship of eleven-year-old Hank Kerner and Bazyli Radichevych (known as Billy Radish), a thirteen-year-old immigrant from Ukraine. Their numerous experiences include seeing older boys go off to war and celebrating Billy's new citizenship, the Fourth of July, and various Ukrainian special days.

Harpoon Island by Pieter VanRaven. New York: Scribner, 1989. [MS] Frank Barnes, a teacher in a one-room schoolhouse on an island off the coast of Maine, learns even more about prejudice in 1917 when the United

States declares war on Germany and the islanders learn of Mr. Barnes's German heritage. The islanders had already shown little tolerance for Mr. Barnes and his small, slow son.

Hero Over Here by Kathleen V. Kudlinski, illustrated by Bert Dodson. New York: Viking, 1990. [I] This story takes place on the American home front during World War I. Ten-year-old Theodore's father and brother are fighting "over there" when the influenza epidemic of 1918 strikes his mother and sister. Teddy becomes a hero "over here" as he cares for his patients until they recover.

Littlejim by Gloria Houston, illustrated by Thomas B. Allen. New York: Philomel, 1990. [I] Set in the Blue Ridge Mountains of North Carolina during World War I, the story is about twelve-year-old gifted Littlejim Houston and his relationship with his father. Littlejim, in an attempt to make his stern and abusive father proud, enters a newspaper essay contest on "What it means to be an American."

No Hero for the Kaiser by Frank Rudolf, translated from the German by Patricia Crampton, illustrated by Klaus Steffens. New York: Lothrop, 1986. [MS] Fourteen-year-old Jan speaks both Polish and German, and after he survives the bombardment of his village in Poland, he joins the German battalion. Though not entirely loyal to the Germans, he and his dog, Fox, do seem to bring them luck as they move from battle to battle on the front in World War I.

War Game by Michael Foreman. New York: Arcade, 1994. [I] Will, Freddie, Lacey, and Billy all enlist in the British army on the same day. The illustrations and text tell the horrors—and a bit of humor—of the war and of the soldiers.

A *Wider Tomorrow* by Margaret Shaw. New York: Holiday, 1990. [MS] This novel is set in England during World War I. The book raises questions about women's rights as it chronicles the life of a grandmother who is successful and her granddaughter who is concerned about her future.

Nonfiction Trade Books

An *Album of World War I* by Dorothy Hoobler and Thomas Hoobler. New York: Watts, 1990. [I] Through historical photographs and short essays, the reader learns about the origins of the war, the Russian Revolution, America's entry into the war, the Versailles Treaty, and more. This excellent pictorial study is a fine introduction to World War I, and to the horrors and devastation of war.

Edith Wilson: The Woman Who Ran the United States by James Giblin, illustrated by Michele Laparte. New York: Viking, 1992. [I] This simple biography tells about Edith Balling Wilson, the widow who married President Woodrow Wilson in 1915 and supported and advised him during World War I. After he suffered a stroke in 1919, she helped run the country so that he wouldn't have to resign and in order for the League of Nations to become a reality.

The Origins of World War I by Stewart Ross. New York: Bookwright Press, 1989. [I] A book in the Witness History series. Includes illustrations, maps, graphs, and brief sketches of leading figures of the war.

World War I by Peter I. Bosco. New York: Facts on File, 1991. [MS] This book is in the America at War series. Photographs and historical facts trace America's involvement in World War I.

World War I Battleship by Richard Humble. New York: Watts, 1989. [I] A book in the Fighting Ships series. It describes life on board the battleship *Dreadnought*, which the British used in World War I.

Express Knowledge

1. Research the many recruiting posters created during World War I. Create your own poster enticing young men of the era to join the United States Army.

2. Make a political cartoon of the beginning of the war or of an event during the war.

3. Reenact the meeting at Versailles of the Big Four.

4. Create a debate between President Wilson and Henry Cabot Lodge about the League of Nations. (They never actually debated, but it would have been interesting if they had.)

5. Draw a map of Europe before and after World War I. In a narrative, describe the changes.

6. Make a chart of Wilson's Fourteen Points.

7. Draw a map of Europe showing the major battle sites.

8. Pretend you are Sergeant Alvin York and give a speech to your classmates about your ideas about the war and how you felt after the war ended.

9. Make a chart indicating how many soldiers died on both sides in World War I.

10. Write slogans promoting the entry of the United States into World War I or slogans advocating that the United States remain neutral.

11. Research and learn the song "Over There," by George M. Cohan.

12. Make a timeline of the major events of World War I.

13. Investigate the lives of personalities such as the Archduke Francis Ferdinand, President Woodrow Wilson, General John J. Pershing, Emperor William II, and Tsar Nicholas II.

Select Topic: World War II

The Great Depression occurred in countries throughout the world, including the United States. It was especially severe in Germany; the Treaty of Versailles that ended World War I had taken land and resources from Germany. Paying more money to the winning nations than Germany could afford created resentment and anger among the German people.

Adolf Hitler took advantage of the situation and promised to improve the lives of Germans. The Nazi Party, led by Hitler, took over the German government. Hitler built an enormous army, preparing for war. In 1939, Germany invaded Poland, which caused France and Britain to declare war on Germany. By 1941, Germany had conquered most of Europe. Benito Mussolini, a dictator in Italy, formed a partnership with Hitler that was known as the Axis. Later, Japan joined forces with them.

As in World War I, the United States wanted to stay out of the war. However, on December 7, 1941, the Japanese attacked the United States naval base at Pearl Harbor in Hawaii. Many Americans lost their lives and many American ships were destroyed. The United States declared war on Japan on the following day. As a result, Germany and Italy then declared war on the United States.

The United States joined forces with Britain, France, the Soviet Union, and other countries to fight the Axis powers. American, British, Canadian, and French forces invaded Normandy and worked their way east across Europe toward Germany. The Soviet Union moved toward Germany from the east. They came together in Germany, crushing the terrible regime. On May 8, 1945, the war finally ended in Europe with Germany's surrender to the Allies.

As the Allied forces conquered Hitler's Germany, they confirmed the rumors that Hitler had committed mass murders of the Jews. In this destruction, which is referred to as the Holocaust, 6.5 million European Jews were killed.

The war with Japan raged on after the war in Europe had ended. As plans were made to invade Japan, it was realized that there would be a huge loss of life for the Allies and for the Japanese people. Therefore, President Harry S. Truman decided to use a new weapon, the atomic bomb. The first atomic bomb was dropped on the city of Hiroshima on August 6, 1945, immediately killing over 100,000 people. A second bomb was dropped on Nagasaki three days later. Neither of the two cities bombed had any major military installations. Soon thereafter, Japan surrendered.

By the end of the war, 13 million Americans were in the military. There were 291,000 Americans killed in battle and over 670,000 wounded. It is estimated that between 40 and 60 million people in the world were killed during the war.

Make Lists and Web

What We Want to Know

- Why did Germany, Italy, and Japan form an alliance in fighting World War II?
- How did Adolf Hitler obtain power in Germany?
- What was the Nazi Party and what did it advocate?
- Why did other countries such as France and England allow Hitler to invade other European countries without attempting to stop him?
- What were the reasons for the success of the German military?
- What weapons were used during the war?
- What caused Joseph Stalin of the Soviet Union to form an alliance with Hitler?
- Why did the United States not enter the war until the bombing of Pearl Harbor?
- How was Britain able to defend itself against Germany?
- Why did Germany invade the Soviet Union and why did the invasion fail?
- Why and how did the Holocaust occur?
- What is the story of Anne Frank and how is it related to World War II?
- How did the United States deal with fighting the war in Europe and in Asia?
- Who were the major military and political leaders in the war and what were their main contributions?
- Why was Japan so successful in its invasion of China and other countries?
- Who were the major military leaders in Europe and in Asia?
- What were some of the major battles in Europe, North Africa, and Asia?
- Why was the invasion of Europe at Normandy successful?

- Why did Japan begin to suffer major setbacks in the war?
- How did the geography of the Pacific region determine war strategies?
- What factors were considered by the Americans in the decision to drop the atomic bomb on Japan?
- What factors weren't considered when the bomb was dropped?
- How did the war affect African Americans?
- How did the war bring new opportunities for women?
- How did racism force Japanese Americans into internment camps?
- What were the consequences for people who committed war crimes?

Subtopics on World War II

- Causes of war
- Holocaust (include persecution of Rom, Slavs, Jehovah's Witnesses, homosexuals, and the mentally ill)
- The alliance of Germany, Italy, and Japan
- Policy of France and Britain toward Germany before the war
- Policy of the United States before the war
- Germany's aggression in Europe
- Britain's defense, including role of Royal Air Force
- Entrance into the war by the United States
- Role of United States military branches, including Waves and Wacs
- Weapons of the war
- Political and military leaders
- Major battles and campaigns in Europe, Asia, and North Africa
- Civilian activities and hardships
- Statistics of the war
- Japan's aggression in the Pacific
- Racism and sexism in the United States
- D-Day
- Atomic bomb
- War criminals
- Japanese internment camps

Form Study Committees and Develop Questions

Questions on the Holocaust

- How many Jews were killed in the Holocaust?
- Why did Hitler hate the Jews and want to destroy all of them?
- How were the Jews murdered?
- Where were the major concentration camps located?
- What happened to the Jews in the concentration camps?
- Who are some famous European Jews and what makes them famous?
- Why didn't more Jewish people flee Europe?
- If they did escape from Europe, where did they go and why?

Study Topic

Fiction Trade Books

Code Name Kris by Carol Matas. New York: Scribner, 1990. [MS] Through flashbacks, a seventeen-year-old tells of his involvement with the Danish resistance movement. One gets a true sense of the bravery of those who fought for the freedom of the Danes.

Hide and Seek by Ida Vos. Boston: Houghton Mifflin, 1991. [I/MS] The author draws on events in her own life to relate a Jewish family's experiences in Holland during the German occupation. Eight-year-old Rachel first begins to note small changes and the disappearance of relatives, and then must go into hiding until the war ends.

Hiroshima: A Novella by Lawrence Yep. New York: Scholastic, 1995. [I/MS] This detailed narrative recounts the events of the day the first atomic bomb was dropped on Hiroshima, the aftermath, and the effects on people, especially on twelve-year-old Sachi. Yep also writes about the destructive potential of nuclear warfare and tells about some of the disarmament efforts now being made.

The Man from the Other Side by Uri Orlev, translated by Hillel Hallin. Boston: Houghton Mifflin, 1991. [I/MS] This excellent coming-of-age novel is set in Poland during World War II. After meeting a young Jewish man, fourteen-year-old Marek helps him to hide in his grandparents' home and becomes involved in the Warsaw ghetto uprising.

My Wartime Summers by Jane Cutler. New York: Farrar Straus, 1994. [I] Both war and preadolescence are explored in this historical novel set during World War II. Pride turns to concern and fear as Ellen's family tracks Uncle Bob's movements in the military.

Sadako by Eleanor Coerr, illustrated by Ed Young. New York: Putnam, 1993. [I] This is a picture book version of Coerr's powerful novel *Sadako and the Thousand Paper Cranes*. This is the true story of a courageous Japanese girl who struggled against leukemia she developed after the bomb attack on Hiroshima.

The Shadow Children by Steven Schnur, illustrated by Herbert Tauss. New York: Morrow, 1994. [I] Ghosts of Jewish children haunt a rural French village after the end of World War II. Fearing for their own safety, the villagers had watched as the Nazis took away the children they had been sheltering.

Summer of My German Soldier by Bette Greene. New York: Dial, 1973. [I/MS] This novel is set in a small town in Arkansas during World War II. A twelve-year-old Jewish girl befriends an escaped German POW, which brings both tragedy and enlightenment to her life.

Waiting for Anya by Michael Morpurgo. New York: Viking, 1991. [I/MS] This action-packed historical novel is set in Vichy, France, during World War II. Twelve-year-old Jo helps Jewish children escape from the German army.

Nonfiction Trade Books

Anne Frank: Beyond the Diary: A Photographic Remembrance by Ruud van der Rol and Rian Verhoeven. New York: Viking, 1993. [MS] In this photo-biography, one learns about Anne's life before the diary and Hitler's rise to power and various events of World War II. Included are interviews with some who knew Anne, and among many photographs is one of the actual diary.

Franklin Delano Roosevelt by Russell Friedman. New York: Clarion, 1990. [I/MS] Through photographs and text, this carefully researched biography portrays the life of FDR and his influence in the world. Includes memorial places to visit.

Hidden Children by Howard Greenfield. New York: Ticknor, 1993. [I] This important book illuminates the plight of Jewish children who were hidden in homes, convents, and institutions during World War II. Greenfield used personal interviews to reinforce his research.

Navajo Code Talkers by Nathan Aaseng. New York: Walker, 1992. [I/MS] Many readers will enjoy learning about the Navajo "code talkers" and the role they played in the United States victory over Japan in World War II. Once a code was created using the Navajo language, it was unbreakable.

Oskar Schindler by Jack L. Roberts. San Diego: Lucent Books, 1996. [MS] A biography about Schindler's life that begins with his youth in Czechoslovakia and follows him through ghettos, to death camps, and the end of his life. Appreciation is gained for the lives of Oskar and Emilie and their assistance to others.

Raoul Wallenberg: The Man Who Stopped Death by Sharon Linnea. New York: Jewish Publication Society, 1993. [MS] Wallenberg, who grew up in Sweden and attended school for a time in America, played an extraordinary role in protecting Hungarian Jews near the end of World War II. Linnea bases her biography on interviews with Wallenberg's contemporaries and on archival documents.

Strange but True Stories of World War II by George Sullivan. New York: Walker, 1991. [I] This reissued book will be of particular interest to World War II buffs. Includes interesting, little-known, and unusual stories of World War II.

We Survived the Holocaust by Elaine Landau. New York: Watts, 1991. [I/MS] Sixteen Holocaust survivors recount their experiences during World War II; many of the survivors were children during the war.

Express Knowledge

1. Make a timeline from 1930 to 1945 showing major acts of aggression by Germany, Italy, and Japan. In addition, show major battles of the war.

2. Pretend that you are Edward R. Murrow (a major U.S. newscaster during World War II). Broadcast major events of the war. You may want to find the scripts of some of his newscasts and use them in your re-creation.

3. Give an oral report to the class about a favorite book you have read on the war, such as *Anne Frank: The Diary of a Young Girl*.

4. Learn about the lives of one or more personalities of the war, including Adolf Hitler, Joseph Stalin, Hideki Tojo, Benito Mussolini, Dwight Eisenhower, Winston Churchill, or Franklin Delano Roosevelt.

5. Plan and perform a mock summit of allied leaders including Roosevelt, Churchill, Charles de Gaulle, and Stalin. Find different crisis situations that occurred during the war to discuss.

6. Research the role of women in the United States armed forces, including their wartime activities, the types of aircraft they flew, and the discrimination they endured. Find explanations for why they had no official military status and thus no benefits.

7. Draw a world map and distinguish the Allied countries with one color, the Axis countries with one color, and the neutral countries with another color. Mark the places where major battles occurred and label them with the name of the battle and the date.

8. Describe how the countries that won the war divided and occupied several countries. How was the Iron Curtain created and then dismantled after World War II?

9. Summarize the actions of the United States government in forming Japanese internment camps. Include your recommendations on how the nation should demonstrate feelings of remorse for the psychological and financial grief caused by the removal of these Asian American citizens from their homes and businesses.

10. Compose poetry to commemorate the lives of millions of European Jewish people whose lives were snuffed out during the Holocaust. Express your feelings about this horrible example of religious persecution.

11. Conduct a study of the sacrifices of ordinary citizens who were not in the military during World War II. Highlight ways in which these people supported the nation during war.

12. Research how the United States financed its part of the war. What were the sources of funds, how was the national debt affected, and how was inflation controlled?

13. Criticize the dictatorships of Adolf Hitler, Benito Mussolini, and General Hideki Tojo. Emphasize the loss of lives, the pain and suffering, and the destruction of the world caused by these men.

Select Topic: Korea, Vietnam, and Desert Storm

The United States has been involved in several different military actions since World War II. The Korean War, Vietnam War, and the Persian Gulf War (Operation Desert Storm) are major military efforts.

All of these military actions were controversial among citizens of the United States for many reasons. Many people felt that civil/regional wars should only be the concern of people inside the country/region; others felt there was no danger to the United States; and many thought the United States shouldn't be the world's peacekeeper.

Make Lists and Web

What We Want to Know

- What were the causes of the conflict?
- Why was the United States involved in the conflict?
- How did the conflict end?
- What happened as a result of the conflict?

Subtopics on Korea, Vietnam, and Desert Storm

- Involvement of the United States
- Involvement of other countries
- Involvement of the United Nations
- Causes of each conflict
- Cost in terms of civilian and military lives
- End of each conflict
- Outcomes of the conflict

Form Study Committees and Develop Questions

Questions on Involvement of the United States

- How did the United States become involved?
- What were major factors in the United States's fighting the war?
- How did the involvement become escalated?
- Why did many Americans oppose our involvement in the conflict?
- How many Americans were killed in the war?
- How did the war end?

Study Topic

Korean War Nonfiction Trade Books

Douglas MacArthur by Jean Darby. Minneapolis: Lerner, 1989. [I] This brief biography sketches the life and career of General MacArthur. His conflict with President Harry Truman over whether to invade China during the Korean War is included.

Harry S. Truman, President by Thomas Fleming. New York: Clarion, 1993. [I] This lively biography is in the Presidential Biography series and has a strong focus on Truman's presidential years. America's involvement in Korea, desegregation of the military, and the establishment of NATO and other history-changing events are included.

The Korean War by Deborah Bachrach. New York: Lucent, 1991. [I/MS] Brief overview of the Korean War. The author examines policies that led to the U.S. involvement and the impact of the war.

The Korean War by Carter Smith. New York: Burdett, 1990. [I] Smith writes about the Korean War, its historical background, and the consequences of the war. This book is in the Turning Points in America series.

Korean War Almanac by Harry G. Summers. New York: Facts on File, 1990. [MS] This detailed discussion of the Korean War is organized alphabetically by topic. Includes an overview, a "dictionary" of events, and a chronology of events.

Vietnam War Fiction Trade Books

And One for All by Theresa Nelson. New York: Orchard Books, 1989. [MS] This is a story of friendship and family relationships during the conflict in Vietnam. It's twelve-year-old Geraldine's story of her older brother, Wing, and his best friend Sam.

Come in from the Cold by Marsha Qualey. Boston: Houghton Mifflin, 1994. [MS] The protest movement brings together Jeff and Maud, two seventeen-year-olds who are both trying to cope with the loss of siblings during the Vietnam War. The two find that life on a commune gives them a sense of hope and security.

Onion Tears by Diana Kidd. New York: Orchard, 1991. [I] Nam-Huong is a refugee from Vietnam who must cope with the horrors she experienced and her traumatic escape from her homeland. With the help of her teacher and letters to a tiny yellow canary she comes to terms with her grief.

Park's Quest by Katherine Paterson. New York: Lodestar, 1988. [MS] Eleven-year-old Park's mother is reluctant to talk about Park's father, who died in Vietnam, and Park learns why when he visits his paternal grandfather. It is there that he meets an assertive Asian girl and learns that they had the same father.

The Purple Heart by Marc Talbert. New York: HarperCollins, 1992. [I/MS] Luke Calvin cannot believe that the tearful and sickly looking man who just returned from Vietnam in 1967 is his war-hero father, so he takes his father's Purple Heart medal and makes up stories to tell his friends. It is only after he loses the medal that he and his father begin to communicate again.

The Wall by Eve Bunting. New York: Clarion, 1990. [I] A young Hispanic boy and his father visit the Vietnam Veterans Memorial in Washington, D.C. They search for and do a tracing of the name of the boy's grandfather, George Munoz, who died in the war.

Vietnam War Nonfiction Trade Books

Always to Remember: The Story of the Vietnam Veterans Memorial by Brent Ashabranner, photographs by Jennifer Ashabranner. New York: Dodd, Mead, 1988. [I] Through poignant text and photographs, this book by the Ashabranners recounts the history of the Vietnam Veterans Memorial. It tells about Jan Scruggs, who spearheaded the drive for a memorial, and Maya Ying Lin, whose design was chosen for the memorial.

America After Vietnam: Legacies of a Hated War by Edward F. Dolan. New York: Watts, 1989. [MS] Dolan presents the long-term problems resulting from the Vietnam War—the damage, both physical and psychological, to the veterans. He discusses MIAs and the immigration of refugees from the war.

America and Vietnam: The Elephant and the Tiger by Albert Marrin. New York: Viking, 1992. [MS] The first few chapters in this excellent book tell the history of Vietnam, the village culture, the rise of Ho Chi Minh, and the splitting of Vietnam into two parts. Marrin makes use of eyewitness accounts and historical photographs as he explores the effects of the war on both countries.

America's Vietnam War: A Narrative History by Elizabeth Becker. New York: Clarion, 1992. [MS] Becker begins this book with a brief history of Vietnam and its relationship to China, France, and other Southeast Asian countries. Events from the 1950s to 1975, when the United States withdrew, including the roles of key government figures in Washington, are analyzed.

An Asian Tragedy: America and Vietnam by David Detzer. Highland Park, NJ: Millbrook, 1992. [MS] An informative history of Vietnam that emphasizes the French and American military involvement over the past fifty years. Many black-and-white war photographs are included.

The Cold War by Michael G. Kort. Brookfield, CT: Millbrook, 1994. [MS] Traces the history of the Cold War from World War II through McCarthyism, the Cuban missile crisis, and Vietnam. It concludes with the collapse of the USSR.

Everett Alvarez, Jr.: A Hero for Our Times by Susan Maloney Clinton. Chicago: Children's Press, 1990. [I] This is the biography of a Mexican American, Everett Alvarez, who was a navy pilot in the Vietnam War. He became the first American prisoner of war in North Vietnam when his plane was shot down in 1963, and remained a POW for nine years before being released.

Portrait of a Tragedy: America and the Vietnam War by James A. Warren. New York: Lothrop, 1990. [I/MS] This book contains a good informative history of America's involvement in the Vietnam War. Includes a selected chronology, a lengthy bibliography, and an index.

Vietnam: A War on Two Fronts by Sidney Lens. New York: Lodestar, 1990. [MS] Tells about the history of U.S. military involvement in Vietnam and the development of the antiwar movement. Lens also points out various illegal and immoral acts by military personnel and government officials.

Vietnam: Why We Fought: An Illustrated History by Dorothy Hoobler and Thomas Hoobler. New York: Knopf, 1990. [MS] Recounts the reasons America went to war in Vietnam, the causes and major events of the war, and why the United States lost. The authors describe a unit on night patrol in the jungle and the treatment of American veterans.

The War in Vietnam by Michael Gibson. New York: Bookwright Press, 1992. [I/MS] A book in the Witness History series. Gibson discusses the history of Vietnam from 1887, including the roles played by France, the United States, the Soviet Union, and others involved in the conflict.

Persian Gulf War Nonfiction Trade Books

Colin Powell: A Man of War and Peace by Carl Senna. Boston: Houghton Mifflin, 1992. [I/MS] This interesting biography documents the rise of Colin Powell, son of hardworking Jamaican immigrants, from childhood to distinguished four-star general and chairman of the Joint Chiefs of Staff. One of the most highly respected men in America, Powell was the strategist behind Desert Storm.

Norman Schwarzkopf: Hero with a Heart by Libby Hughes. New York: Dillon, 1992. [I] This well-researched biography with black-and-white photographs is part of the People in Focus series. Schwarzkopf graduated from West Point, served in Vietnam, took part in the invasion of Grenada, and became a hero during the Persian Gulf War.

War in the Persian Gulf by Fred Bratman. Brookfield, CT: Millbrook, 1991. [I] An account of the Persian Gulf War from the Iraqi invasion of Kuwait to the allied victory in 1991. Photographs and graphics enhance this informative text.

Express Knowledge

1. Write a letter to the editor that supports the involvement of the United States in the war. Write another letter that states reasons for not being involved.

2. Find a song written in the 1960s to protest the Vietnam War. Research the lyrics and perform the song.

3. Imagine that you are a speechwriter for President Truman in 1950. Write a speech for him that justifies his reason for deciding to resist when North Korea invaded South Korea.

4. Write an essay that explains why President Truman fired General MacArthur during the Korean War. Include your views on the firing.

5. Make a brief report to the class on what you found about the effects of napalm and defoliants used during the Vietnam War.

6. Explain why the Vietnam War was the source of so much controversy in the United States. Present some of the arguments stated in the United States Congress during the time of the war.

7. Draw a map of the world and mark all the places where United States armed troops have served since the Revolutionary War.

8. Predict places in the world where you feel conflict could erupt and places that have current conflicts that could escalate. Also predict the views of United States citizens, the United Nations, and other countries if troops were sent.

9. Select one military action since World War II and survey the attitudes of family and community members about the United States's involvement. Construct a chart that conveys the results of the survey.

10. Compare and contrast two military actions since World War II. Consider the number of lives lost, the costs, and the destruction of the environment.

Resources
Professional Books for Teachers

The following books have been selected to support you as you deepen your knowledge about human and military conflict and to assist you in developing your curriculum. Some books may contain information you can share with students by reading aloud or by sharing sections of the book.

BACHRACH, S. 1994. *Tell Them We Remember*. Boston: Little, Brown.

CRARY, E. 1984. *Kids Can Cooperate*. Seattle: Parenting Press.

DREW, N. 1987. *Learning the Skills of Peacemakers*. Torrance, CA: Jalmar Press.

GIBBS, J. 1995. *Tribes*. Santa Rosa, CA: Center Source Systems Publications.

KREIDLER, W. 1994. *Creative Conflict Resolution*. Glenview, IL: Scott Foresman.

LAWLISS, C. 1991. *The Civil War Source Book*. New York: Harmony Books.

LEFEVRE, D. 1988. *New Games for the Whole Family*. New York: Putnam.

MELTZER, M. 1987. *The American Revolutionaries: A History in Their Own Words*. New York: Harper and Row.

———. 1989. *Voices from the Civil War.* Washington, DC: Library of Congress.

MORRIS, R. B. 1985. *The American Revolution.* Minneapolis: Lerner Publications.

Personnel of the Civil War. 1961. New York: Thomas Yoseloff.

PRUTZMAN, P., L. STERN, M. BURGER, AND G. BODENHAMER. 1988. *The Friendly Classroom for a Small Planet.* Philadelphia: New Society Publications.

SODALLA, G., ET AL. 1990. *Conflict Resolution: An Elementary Curriculum.* San Francisco: National Research Center.

TIME-LIFE BOOKS. 1990. *Brother Against Brother.* Englewood Cliffs, NJ: Prentice-Hall.

TOTTEN, S. 1995. *Select Bibliography—Holocaust Literature.* Fayetteville, AR: University of Arkansas.

WALTER, V. 1993. *War and Peace Literature for Children and Young Adults: A Resource Guide to Significant Issues.* Phoenix: Zephyr.

Documents

Many primary source materials are available, so that students can see a copy of the original document and read the actual text or see photographs and prints of an event. The following list represents some places to find primary sources. Many of the addresses are in the list at the end of this chapter or the list in Appendix A.

- Government Printing Office
  Historical Register of the United States Army (two volumes listing officers of the North and South with names of popular regiments)

- Historical societies (state and local)
  Information about military places of interest, war personalities, photograph collections, microfilm of newspapers, diaries, histories, and many primary sources

- National Archives, Educational Division
  Catalogs that include military documents such as the "muster rolls" or adjutant general reports (listing of soldier's name and age, place where soldier enlisted and mustered, who enlisted him/her, regiment and military engagements)

- National Archives, Library of Congress
  Reproductions of military maps and reproductions of posters and postcards from World Wars I and II

- Smithsonian Museum
  Information concerning the military involvement of United States troops

Selected Print

There are so many different series and individual books available that it is impossible to list all of them. We have included several that we would use in TIs.

- Cobblestone Publishing Company
  Journals *Faces* and *Calliope*, with current and back issues on military conflicts
- Facts on File
  Who Was in the Civil War? by Stewart Sifakos, 1988.
- Greenhaven Press Inc.
  Several series of materials include: Opposing Viewpoints Junior series: *Causes of Crime*, *Death Penalty*, *Gun Control*, *Prisons*, and *Child Abuse*; Overview series: *Death Penalty*, *Family Violence*, *Gun Control*, *Child Abuse*, *Gangs*, and *Hate Groups*; The Way People Live series: *Life in War-Torn Bosnia* and *Life in the Warsaw Ghetto*; The Great Battles in History series: *Battle of Gettysburg*, *Battle of Britain*, *Battle of Midway*, *Invasion of Normandy*, and *Inchon Invasion*; The America's Wars series: discusses all United States wars, including the Persian Gulf War; World History series: *The French and Indian War* and *Hitler's Reich*
- Historical Times Inc.
  Publication titled *Civil War Times* and other issues
- Jackdaw Publications
  Teaching with Historical Places includes teaching units on the *North American Battlegrounds* of World War II, *First Battle of Manassas*, *An End to Innocence: Andersonville Prisoner of War Camp*, *Remembering Pearl Harbor: The U.S.S. Arizona Memorial*, *A Bastion of America's Eastern Seaboard: Fort Pickens and the Outbreak of the Civil War*, *Guilford Courthouse: A Pivotal Battle in the War for Independence*, *The Battle of Stones River: The Soldiers' Story*, *The Battle of Bunker Hill: Now We Are at War*, *Choices and Commitments: The Soldiers at Gettysburg*, *Chatam Plantation: Witness to the Civil War*, and *The Battle of Horseshoe Bend: Collisions of Cultures*
- Kendall/Hunt Publishing Co.
  Women in Industry: World War II. Dubuque, IA, 1991. (letters, pictures, cartoons, pamphlets, memoranda, and executive order concerning the role of women in industry)

Media

Many wonderful videotapes, audio recordings, maps, posters, and much more are available from a variety of resources. We have listed a few that we have examined, but many more exist.

- Cable History Channel
  Weekly programming including war productions for viewing or recorded for educational use

- Knowledge Unlimited
  Revolutionary and Civil War battle maps, posters, videocassettes, CD-ROM on United States wars
- Millbrook Publishing Company
  Gateway Civil Rights series, which includes *James Meredith and School Desegregation*, *Antilynching Crusade and the Freedom Riders*, and *Power of Organized Protest*
- Public Broadcasting Service
  Catalog listings of documentary series and individual videos on many wars, including Ken Burns's *The Civil War* (1991)
- Recorded Books, Inc.
  Taped books include *April Morning* (Howard Fast), *Day of Infamy* (Howard Lord), *Hiroshima* (John Hersey), *Johnny Tremain* (Esther Forbes), *The Red Badge of Courage* (Stephen Crane), *Summer of My German Soldier* (Bette Greene), *The Boy and the Samurai* (Eric C. Haugqaard), and *The Fighting Ground* (Avi)
- SSSS (Social Studies School Series)
  Large collection of media related to all wars in United States history, including videos such as *Vietnam: A Television History* and many more

Technology
Use of the computer expands each day; therefore, it is impossible to list current individual programs and World Wide Web sites.

- World Wide Web sites—maps, photographs, and interviews on most wars
- Internet/e-mail—correspondence with others who are interested in topics on conflict

People
Almost every community has individuals who are knowledgeable on a TI topic. They can be found near the school (parents, staff members, and community members), in private and public agencies, and at local universities and colleges. We have listed some of the people we would invite to speak to our students. Interpersonal conflict and intergroup conflict resources people include:

- Government officials (mayor, city council members, sheriff's office employees, chief-of-police representatives)
- Judicial officers (judges, lawyers, probation officers)
- Reentry groups that support former prisoners

- Parole officers
- Leaders of civil rights organizations
- Individuals who have worked for equal rights

Military conflict resource people include:

- Veterans (male and female)
- Current members of the military forces
- Local war historians
- History teachers from local colleges, universities, and secondary schools
- People who stage mock reenactments, encampments, and battles
- Community residents who lived through wars in other countries

Interview Question Ideas

The following interview questions are meant to be a beginning point as your students develop questions of their own.

Interview Questions About Interpersonal Conflict

- What are some of the ways you recommend solving conflicts?
- What are ways to help people be less violent?
- Do you recommend one specific type of conflict management? If so, will you tell me about it?
- Why do you think there are so many people who are violent in conflict situations?
- Do you know any people who were violent who learned to control their emotions? Can you give some examples?
- What are your views concerning current gun control regulations?
- What is your opinion about the manner in which the judicial system handles violent individuals?

Interview Questions About Intergroup Conflict

- Why do you think different groups of people in the United States do not value each other?
- What are some of the reasons that some groups of people give for not respecting other groups of people?
- Do you know any leaders in the civil rights movement?
- Do you understand their position concerning civil rights?
- What groups other than ethnic minorities have had difficulty realizing their equal rights?

- What do you think are some of the solutions to the problems of equal and civil rights?
- Do you think that the laws that have been passed to protect different groups of people have accomplished their goals?
- What gains have been made in the United States regarding equal and civil rights?

Interview Questions for Veterans

- How did you become involved in the conflict?
- Were you drafted or did you enlist?
- How many others from your community were involved in the war?
- What did you do during the war?
- What did you eat?
- What did you wear?
- Where did you sleep?
- How did you travel?
- Did you march with other soldiers? If so, how many pounds did you carry?
- How were you treated when you returned home?
- Did you receive any injuries? How?
- Did you know anyone who was injured or killed? Who and how?
- Did you know anyone who was a prisoner of war?
- What messages did you receive from your family and friends?
- What songs were sung during the war?
- Do you remember any slogans that were related to the war?
- How did the fighting affect you?
- Did you have any postwar stress?
- What were the harmful effects of the war?
- How do you feel today about what happened during the war?

Interview Questions for Community Members Who Lived Through a War in Another Country or the United States

- What war did you live through?
- How were you affected by the war?
- Did any of your family members go to war?
- How many members of the armed forces from your community went to war?

- Did they enlist or were they drafted?
- Did you know anyone who was wounded or died?
- What were the effects of the war on your life?
- Did you do anything to help with the war?
- Do you remember any of the news coverage of the war?
- Why did the United States become involved in the war?
- What do you think the moral obligation of the United States was in connection with the war?
- Do you remember anything the president of the United States said during the war?

Interview Questions to Use with Individuals Who Stage Mock Reenactments of Encampments and Battles

- How did you become interested in the historical event?
- How did you research the actual event?
- Do you know what aspects of the mock event are historically accurate?
- If some aspects of the mock event aren't accurate, which events are they and why is it not possible to be accurate?
- Where did you get your equipment and weapons?
- Where did you get your costumes?
- When do you stage your mock event?
- What types of people are interested in observing a mock reenactment?

Family History

Family and oral history research are very similar in the way they are conducted. We have listed them separately but we encourage you to refer to the information in both sections. Refer to Appendix E for information on conducting family history research.

Military Conflict

Many students have family members who served in military conflicts or who stayed home when others went to war. Recording the memories of family members is a lasting gift for future generations.

Interviewing family members about their involvement in wars or military actions can be an important aspect of family history. First, find out if any family members are veterans of any wars or were alive during World War I, World War II, or recent wars. Arrange a time when you can interview them. Many of the questions that are included in the interview section can be used. Tape-record the interview; transcribe and edit the text to serve as a written history.

Many families have letters, photographs, diaries, uniforms, newspaper clippings, medals, certificates, flags, weapons, and other artifacts. Make photographs and photocopies of the prized possessions that can be shared with future generations.

Civil Rights

Some families have members who have been active in the civil rights or equal rights movement in the United States. Documenting a family's participation and contribution to the improvement of life in the United States is a gift for that person and all others who read the text.

Some of the suggested interview questions can be used if you are able to find a family member to talk to you. The interview can be tape-recorded and transcribed for future reading. Photographs or newspaper clippings can be copied and added to the interview transcription.

Oral History

Oral history ideas are included that can be photocopied and given to students to serve as a springboard for the development of their questions. Because oral and family history have similarities, we encourage you to read the family history section above. Refer to Appendix E for information on how to conduct oral history research.

Oral history is finding information from the entire community. Engaging in oral history research enables future citizens in the community to fully appreciate those who came before them.

Look for individuals who have served in a war, lived in the community during the war, or made a contribution to the civil or equal rights movement. The list of resource people can be the beginning pool because people who are knowledgeable often have had personal experience. One example would be to find community members who remember the building of war monuments in your area.

Field Trips

In many communities, students can visit places to gain a deeper understanding of a topic. This list represents places we would want to take students during a TI. We suggest that in addition to planning class field trips, you also might develop a list of places where families could visit. The list could be sent home as part of a letter to parents (see Appendix D for parent letter ideas).

- Mock reenactments of battles and encampments
- Veterans' monuments and memorials

- Military cemeteries
- Local cemeteries with marked veterans' graves
- Veterans Administration hospitals and nursing homes
- Native American, Civil War, or other battlegrounds
- Museums (public and private)
- Local or state historical society buildings
- War historian's office or home
- Army, Air Force, Navy, Marine, Coast Guard bases
- Living history parks
- Art galleries (paintings of battles, etc.)
- Places concerning interpersonal and intergroup conflict
- Police stations
- Family court
- Juvenile detention centers

Art

There are many examples of the visual arts in most communities, such as murals in public places, paintings and drawings in museums, sculptures in military museums or parks, monuments in city squares, parks, or cemeteries, and prints of military scenes and personalities in private collections.

Students like to draw before-and-after battle scenes and sketch different kinds of weapons and military uniforms.

- *American Artists Reflect American History Series*, Vol. III, Revolutionary Times, and Vol. IV, Civil War Era, Creative Teaching Press, Cypress, CA 90630 (works of art reproduced with information about artists)

- *The American Revolution*, American Library Color Slide Company, P.O. Box 5810, Grand Central Station, NY 10163–5810 (set of twenty-five slides of paintings of war)

- *The European Vision of America* from National Gallery of Art Extension Services, Washington, DC 20565 (audiocassette and eighteen slides of European artists' visions of America)

- I *Never Saw Another Butterfly: Children's Drawings and Poems from Terezin Concentration Camp*, 1942–1944. 1993. New York: Schocken Books (drawings and poems by children written during their incarceration)

- *National Archives Trust Fund Catalog* (reproductions of posters and postcards from World Wars I and II)

Music

Numerous songs have been written about wars. Many general anthologies include a section on wars, and some war songs are listed under different periods in history. The Smithsonian Collection of Recordings is one excellent source. Public libraries often have a shelf of old and new song books, a collection of sheet music, and sound recordings that include war songs. Reading the words to the songs can reveal feelings about the war that aren't included in text. Often the songs began as poems that were set to music. Several collections that are valuable include the following:

Birth of Liberty: Music of the American Revolution, from *Recorded Anthology of American Music*, New World Records (primary source which includes fife and drum corps and songs)

GLASS, PAUL. 1975. *Singing Soldiers: A History of the Civil War in Song*. New York: Grossett & Dunlap.

Mud and Stars: An Anthology of World War Songs and Poetry. 1931. New York: Henry Holt.

RICHARDS, LAURA E., collector. 1918. *To Arms: Songs of the Great Wars*. Boston: Page Company.

SCOTT, JOHN A. 1972. *Ballad of America: The History of the United States in Song and Story*. New York: Bantam Pathfinders Edition. (Chapter 5 deals with music from the Civil War, and other chapters have songs from other wars.)

WHITMAN, WANDA W., ed. 1969. *Songs That Changed the World*. New York: Crown. (Includes three hundred of the most influential songs in the course of history.)

Some favorite Civil War songs include "John Brown's Body," "Battle Hymn of the Republic," "Tenting on the Old Camp Ground," "When Johnny Comes Marching Home," "The Battle Cry of Freedom," and "Marching Through Georgia."

Addresses

The addresses in this section are provided because each is a source for information or materials related to the TIs on conflict outlined in this book. Additional addresses can be found in Appendix A. (Please check the *Encyclopedia of Associations* found at many public libraries for most current addresses.)

American Legion, 700 Pennsylvania Street, Indianapolis, IN 46204

American-Arab Anti-Discrimination Committee, 4201 Connecticut Avenue, N.W., Suite 500, Washington, DC 20008

Army Association of the United States, 2425 Wilson Boulevard, Arlington, VA 22201

Center for Defense Information, 1500 Massachusetts Avenue, N.W., Washington, DC 20005

Constitutional Rights Foundation, 601 South Kingsley Drive, Los Angeles, CA 90005

Daughters of the American Revolution, 1776 D Street, N.W., Washington, DC 20006-5392

Daughters of the Confederacy, 328 North Boulevard, Richmond, VA 23220-4057

Daughters of the War of 1812, 1461 Rhode Island Avenue, N.W., Washington, DC 20005

Daughters of Union Veterans of the Civil War, 503 Walnut Street, Springfield, IL 62704

Department of Defense, The Pentagon 20301, Washington, DC 20005

Department of Veterans' Affairs, 810 Vermont Avenue, N.W., Washington, DC 20420

Ex-Prisoners of War, 3201 East Pioneer Parkway #40, Arlington, TX 75010-5396

General Society of Colonial Wars, 840 Woodbine Avenue, Glendale, OH 45246

Institute for Peace and Justice, 4144 Lindell, Room 122, St. Louis, MO 63108

Korean War Veterans Memorial, 18th & C Streets, N.W., Room 7424, Washington, DC 20240-9997

Lion and Lamb Peace Arts Center, Bluffton College, Bluffton, OH 45817

Military Order of the World Wars, 435 North Lee Street, Alexandria, VA 22314

National Register of Historic Places, Interagency Resources Division, National Park Service, U.S. Dept. of the Interior, P.O. Box 37127, Washington, DC 20013-7127

National Street Law Institute, 605 G Street, N.W., Washington, DC 20001

Peace Education Foundation, Inc. 3550 Biscayne Boulevard, Suite 400, Miami, FL 33137-3854

Pearl Harbor Survivors Association, 3215 Albert Street, Orlando, FL 32816

Resources for Nonviolence, 515 Broadway, Santa Cruz, CA 95060

Study for Prevention of Violence, 3109 Mayfield Road, Cleveland Heights, OH 44118

Veterans of Foreign Wars of the U.S., 406 West 34th Street, Kansas City, MO 64111

Veterans of the Vietnam War, 760 Jumper Road, Wilkes-Barre, PA 18702-9033

Veterans of World War I, 941 North Capitol Street, N.E., Room 1201-C, Washington, D.C. 20002-4234

Women World War Veterans, 237 Madison Avenue, New York, NY 10016

Young Americans for Freedom, 140 18A Sullyfield Circle, Chantilly, VA 22021

Settlement of the United States

3

Settlement on land that is now known as the United States began slowly. Europeans settled on the East Coast, pushing the Native Americans farther inland. Slaves were brought to the colonies, primarily to those in the South, to work the large plantations. The thirteen colonies that were formed were tied to England. In the late 1700s, the colonists rebelled against England, fighting and winning the Revolutionary War. Thus, the world saw the birth of a new nation—the United States of America.

In the 1800s, with the purchase of the Louisiana Territory from France, the size of the United States was doubled. There were skirmishes between the settlers and the Native Americans, and there was the Civil War. Immigrants poured in from all over the world.

There is much to know about the settlement of the United States of America, and there are many different perspectives. It is an important topic that requires in-depth study over a long period of time to adequately understand.

Needless to say, we have not included all of the important topics regarding the settlement of the United States—not even the most important facts. It has been our objective to provide a framework for teachers to help students study settlement using themes and a variety of resources rather than a textbook-bound approach. In this section, we suggest ideas for themes on the settlement of the United States, dividing settlement into four time frames: (1) before Jamestown; (2) Jamestown through the end of the Revolutionary War; (3) after the Revolutionary War through the end of the Civil War; and (4) after the Civil War to the beginning of World War I.

Select Topic: Before Jamestown

The first people in North America probably came from Asia thousands of years ago. These Native Americans lived on the North American continent long before the Europeans arrived. They were organized into hundreds of tribes and bands; each had its own language, religion, government, and customs.

The first Europeans to explore the North American continent were probably the Viking explorers, who found large numbers of fish in the Grand Banks off North America. Later, Columbus made Europeans aware of this great continent when he landed in the West Indies in an attempt to find a new route to China.

After Columbus, several European countries explored the New World. Many settlements were developed years before the settlement of Jamestown in 1607.

Make Lists and Web

If you and your students have selected the topic "Before Jamestown," the next step is to assess your students' prior knowledge by asking them to tell what they know about our country before Jamestown was founded. We suggest a whole-class brainstorming session in which you make a list of what they know on a transparency or on the chalkboard. After this list is completed, encourage the class to ask questions about what they would like to know. The following may help you and your students make your own lists of "What we want to know."

What We Want to Know

- Who were the first known European explorers of the North American continent?
- What happened as a result of the early explorations?
- Who were the first known inhabitants of North America? How and when did they arrive?
- What was the lifestyle of Native Americans before the arrival of the Europeans? How were their cultures similar and different?
- What role did the geographic conditions play in the development of the Native American cultures?
- Why did Europeans settle in North America?
- What contributed to the conquest of the Native Americans?
- What European countries were dominant in the early settlement of the continent? Why?
- What were some of the exchanges of ideas, customs, food products, animals, and diseases?

After the class has thought about what they want to know and the questions are formulated, it is time to organize the study. Ask the students to review all of their questions in order to develop a list of subtopics that represent the questions. Remind them that one question often relates to more than one subtopic. In the large group, guide students to generate a list. The following subtopics might give you ideas as you and your students make your own list.

Subtopics on Settlement Before Jamestown

- Early exploration and settlement
- Cultures of the Native Americans
- Geographic conditions and effects on the Native Americans and Europeans
- Causes for European exploration and settlement
- Conquest of the Native Americans
- Exchange of information, etc., between the Europeans and the Native Americans

After the subtopics have been decided, a web can be constructed. Web the major subtopics that you and the students have identified and then add subordinate ideas to the subtopics. You will probably web on the chalkboard or overhead and then copy the final web on paper so that students can later refer to it.

Form Study Committees

After completing a web, the students should be organized into study committees. You and the students need to decide with whom students will work in their small groups and what topics they prefer to research. If you have a group of twenty-four students, for example, you might form six groups with four students in each group. In this case, you might limit the number of subtopics to six, with each group studying one of the subtopics.

Develop Questions

Students must be interested enough in a topic to raise questions and explore those questions through research. Ask each group to develop as many questions on the subtopic as they can and to record them on a blank transparency. They can later share them with the rest of the class and hear their comments.

For example, if you have a study committee on early exploration and settlement, they might raise some of the following questions, or you might suggest that they research some of these questions.

Questions on Early Exploration and Settlement

- Where did Spain establish settlements? France? England?
- Why?
- Who were the major explorers? What did they do?
- What did settlements look like?
- How long did the settlements last?
- What were the problems that the explorers faced?
- Why were the Europeans looking for new trade routes?
- What was occurring in Europe at the time of the early explorations in the 1400s and 1500s?

Study Topic

Once students have identified questions relevant to their topic, they begin their study. As students engage in study, they will add questions and delete some of their original ones. They use many resources, including books, nonprint sources, magazines and newspapers, and computers. We suggest several books in this section and indicate whether they are appropriate for intermediate (I) or middle school (MS) students. In the reference section at the end of this chapter, we include other appropriate resources.

Fiction Trade Books

Morning Girl by Michael Dorris. New York: Hyperion, 1992. [I/MS] Morning Girl, who likes to greet the morning, and Star Boy, her brother, who prefers events of the night, are Taino children living in the West Indies in the late fifteenth century. Alternating chapters, narrated by brother and sister, reveal much about the people whose lives are about to be disrupted forever when Morning Girl goes to find the village leaders to greet the canoe filled with strangers in 1492.

The Very First Thanksgiving: Pioneers on the Rio Grande by Bea Bragg, illustrated by Antonio Bragg. Melbourne, FL: Harbinger House, 1989. [I] In 1598, Don Juan de Oñate led an expedition of four hundred people and seven thousand animals from Mexico to Texas. The journey was fraught with hardships, but upon their arrival at the Rio Grande near present-day El Paso, the Spanish travelers held a feast of celebration with the local native peoples.

Nonfiction Trade Books

Ancient America by Marion Wood. New York: Facts on File, Inc., 1989. [I] Maps, color photographs, and concise overviews of the history and culture of native groups are provided. Includes culture, geographic conditions, and artifacts.

Christopher Columbus: Voyager to the Unknown by Nancy Smiler Levinson. New York: Lodestar, 1990. [I] This detailed description of Columbus's four voyages emphasizes the different perspectives historians can consider when telling the story of Columbus. Includes letters of authorization, names of crew members, and a chronology of events.

Coming to America: Immigrants from the British Isles by Shirley Blumenthal and Jerome S. Ozer. New York: Dell, 1980. [I] Tells about the first group of immigrants to come to American shores. Illustrated with photographs and prints.

The Discoverers of America by Harold Faber. New York: Scribner, 1992. [MS] Faber presents a comprehensive picture of the exploration and settlement of the American continent from Alaska to Cape Horn in South America. Many explorers' voyages are included.

The Discovery of the Americas by Renardo Barden. San Diego: Greenhaven Press, 1989. [I/MS] Part of the Great Mysteries: Opposing Viewpoints series, this book puts Columbus's explorations in historical context. The author presents historical and archaeological evidence of Viking and other possible visitors, including prehistoric sailors, to the Americas.

The Discovery of the Americas by Betsy and Giulio Maestro. New York: Lothrop, 1991. [I/MS] The authors recount the early settlement and exploration of the Americas from 20,000 B.C. to 1522 and briefly describe voyages of each of the major explorers. The book includes useful maps and a timeline.

The Earliest Americans by Helen Roney Sattler, illustrated by Jean Day Zallinger. New York: Clarion, 1993. [I] Explores a variety of theories about the earliest inhabitants of the Western Hemisphere. Who were the earliest Americans? Where did they come from? When did they arrive? These questions and more are examined in this fascinating book.

The Explorers and Settlers: A Sourcebook on Colonial America by Carter Smith (editor). Highland Park, NJ: Millbrook Press, 1991. [MS] Part of the American Albums from the Collections of the Library of Congress series, this book is primarily a pictorial history of the exploration and colonization of the United States from 1492 to 1775. Captions and detailed timelines provide a good overview of the time period.

How We Learned the Earth Is Round by Patricia Lauber, illustrated by Megan Lloyd. New York: HarperCollins, 1990. [I] Recounts 2,500 years of exploration. Focuses on contributions of the Greeks, Columbus, and Magellan.

I, Columbus: My Journal—1492–3 by Peter Roop and Connie Roop (editors), illustrated by Peter Hanson. New York: Walker, 1990. [I] A useful introduction to Columbus's explorations. Excerpts from his journal tell of his first voyage to the New World.

The Penguin Atlas of North American History to 1870 by Colin McEvedy. New York: Penguin, 1986. [I] This historical atlas is a good resource for classroom research.

People of the Breaking Day by Marcia Sewall. New York: Atheneum, 1990. [I] This poetic text is a story of the Wampanoag Indians who were living in southeastern Massachusetts when the Pilgrims arrived. The realistic paintings work well with the text to portray the lives of these people.

The Tainos: The People Who Welcomed Columbus by Francine Jacobs, illustrated by Patrick Collins. New York: Putnam, 1992. [I/MS] The Tainos were the indigenous people who lived in the Greater Antilles in the Caribbean and peacefully welcomed Columbus on his arrival in 1492. Jacobs describes the cruelty, greed, and barbarism of the European explorers.

Who Discovered America? Mysteries and Puzzles of the New World by Patricia Lauber, illustrated by Mike Eagle. New York: HarperCollins, 1992. [I] Lauber outlines the travels and discoveries of early Siberian hunters who crossed the Bering land bridge, Asian fishermen who were in Ecuador, and the Vikings. Maps and pen-and-ink drawings accompany the text.

Who Discovered America? Settlers and Explorers of the New World Before the Time of Columbus by Patricia Lauber. New York: Random House, 1970. [I] A "scientific" detective story. Specialists investigate clues to tell the story of the New World before Columbus's time.

Express Knowledge

1. Research the different theories about how and when American Indians and the Eskimos settled North America. Prepare an oral presentation comparing/contrasting your findings.

2. Draw a picture that depicts some aspect of Native American life before the Europeans came to the Americas.

3. Create a map showing North and South America, Europe, and Africa. Using different colored pens, trace the four voyages of Columbus to the Americas. You might want to do the same thing with other early explorers. Compare/contrast voyages and reasons for the exploration of America.

4. Study the opinions of different historians about Christopher Columbus. Find two sources that are in conflict and outline how they differ, including different accounts about Columbus's purpose for exploring and the location of his landings.

5. Investigate the different explorers who sailed to North America before English settlement. Make maps showing where they were in North America and record the reports they gave in Europe about their experiences.

6. Study the Lost Colony at Roanoke and the mystery surrounding the fate of the settlers. Hypothesize why the settlement failed and the fate of the vanished settlers.

7. Devise a chart that shows the early settlements, when and where they were founded, and the founding country.

8. Read about Leif Eriksson and other Viking explorers and fishermen. Discuss with other students why news of their discoveries wasn't known by most people in Europe.

9. Construct a model of a Viking sailing ship. Write a description of the ship and the Vikings.

10. Pretend that you were on the ship of Columbus or on one of the ships of another early explorer. Write a letter back home describing the trip.

11. Make an illustrated timeline that shows the dates when explorers arrived from 1492 to 1607.

12. Write a brief report on one or more of the early explorers.

13. Analyze the settlement of North America from a Native American perspective. Share the results of the analysis in a written or oral report.

14. Compare the settlement policies and practices of several European countries. Share the differences and similarities in chart form.

15. Hypothesize how the settlement of North America would have been different if one European country had taken a different course of action or policy toward North America. Write a decree that a European king, queen, or emperor might have issued.

16. Write a position paper about your beliefs on what happened to the Native Americans in the settlement of North America.

17. Imagine current and future explorations of Antarctica, the ocean, and space. Is there any similarity between this modern exploration and the settlement of the United States? Write a summary of your thinking.

Select Topic: Jamestown (1607) to 1783

Many people from England settled in North America during the 1600s and 1700s. In 1607, Jamestown was founded; it was the first successful English colony in North America. Later, other colonies were founded in the 1600s, including Massachusetts, Maryland, and the Carolinas. Georgia, the last of the British colonies, was founded in 1732.

The New England colonies grew rapidly, and by the 1700s there were many types of skilled and professional workers, including merchants, sailors, and farmers. Boston had a population of fifteen thousand by 1750.

The middle colonies also prospered. In addition to the English settlers, thousands of immigrants arrived from Germany and other European countries. Farms in the middle colonies prospered and produced abundant amounts of grain. The area soon became known as the breadbasket of the New World. Philadelphia and New York became important centers of trade and business.

The southern colonies had rich soil and a mild climate, which enabled the area to produce large amounts of crops to sell to England and other countries. The main cash crop was tobacco; cotton became an important cash crop much later. Since there were many large plantations in the southern colonies, many workers were needed. Thus, slaves were brought from Africa to work on the plantations.

In the latter half of the eighteenth century, the colonists objected to British rule. The colonists did not want to pay the taxes forced on them by the British; they refused to accept "taxation without representation." Thus, the colonists declared their independence from Great Britain. The Revolutionary War is not included in this TI because it is addressed as a separate TI in Chapter 2.

Make Lists and Web

What We Want to Know

- Why did people want to come to America?
- What were the conditions on the ship like for people coming to America?
- What was the Mayflower Compact?
- Who were the Pilgrims?
- Where were the early settlements? What was life like in the early settlements?
- What political, social, and religious beliefs did the colonists hold?
- What were Britain's reasons for wanting the colonies?

- Who was an indentured servant?
- Why was all the land owned by the king of England?
- Why was slavery so prominent in the southern colonies?
- What were the French and Indian wars?
- How did the middle colonies differ from one another?
- Who were leaders in the colonies?
- What was education like in the colonies?

Subtopics on the Colonies from Jamestown to 1783

- Condition of life in the colonies
- Reasons for people to go to the colonies
- Leaders in the colonies
- Indentured servitude
- Slavery
- Conditions in countries from which the colonists came
- Political, social, and religious beliefs of the early colonists
- Role of women
- Role of children
- Relationship of the colonists with the Native Americans
- Similarities and differences among the colonies
- Governance of the colonies
- Economy of the colonies
- Education in the colonies
- Religion of the colonists
- Major documents
- Slavery

Form Study Committees and Develop Questions

Questions on the Condition of Life in the Colonies

- What did the colonists eat?
- How did they clothe themselves?
- What kind of work did they do?
- Did they exchange money or did they exchange goods to pay for things?
- What kind of housing did they have?
- What happened when they became ill?

- What kinds of laws did they have to govern themselves?
- Did they have churches?
- What were their schools like?

Study Topic

Fiction Trade Books

Beyond the Burning Time by Kathryn Lasky. New York: Blue Sky, 1994. [MS] Lasky re-creates the Salem witch trials in this passionately told story. Twelve-year-old Mary Chase's reaction and her mother's trial make for a real page-turner.

Charlie's House by Clyde Robert Bulla. New York: Scribner, 1983. [I] An indentured servant and then a runaway, twelve-year-old Charlie Brig is outspoken and independent. This book provides insights into a child's role in the eighteenth century in both England and the New World.

Constance: A Story of Early Plymouth by Patricia Clapp. New York: Puffin, 1986. [MS] This novel, set in Plymouth, Massachusetts, tells about the Pilgrims' first six years in the Plymouth settlement. The story is told in journal format through the eyes of Constance, who was not happy about her family's move to the New World on the *Mayflower*.

Encounter at Easton by Avi. New York: Morrow, 1994. [I] Avi sets this novel in colonial Pennsylvania and focuses on two runaway indentured servants, Robert Linnly and Elizabeth Mawes. The book is written in the form of court testimony by Robert and others.

The Fifth of March: A Story of the Boston Massacre by Ann Rinaldi. San Diego: Gulliver, 1993. [MS] Boston in 1770 is the setting for this book in the American Colonies series. Rachel Marsh is an indentured servant to John and Abigail Adams and has firsthand knowledge of the family's struggles and of the tensions in Boston.

I Am Regina by Sally M. Keehn. New York: Philomel, 1991. [MS] This is a first-person fictionalized account of Regina Leininger, who was captured by Native Americans in 1755 and held until 1763. They adopted her into their family and she tells about her years with them and how she regretted leaving them when returned to her former life.

Paul Revere's Ride by Henry Wadsworth Longfellow, illustrated by Ted Rand. New York: Dutton, 1990. [I] Beautiful full-color illustrations bring to life and capture the drama of the famous midnight ride. One can almost hear the horses' hoofs as the townspeople of Massachusetts were warned of the coming of the British.

Saturnalia by Paul Fleischman. New York: HarperCollins, 1990. [I/MS] William, a fourteen-year-old Narraganset Indian who was earlier captured by whites, is contentedly indentured to a painter and his family, but must decide whether to return to his tribe or stay in Boston. The story contains some humor and provides a portrait of Boston in 1681.

The Serpent Never Sleeps: A Novel of Jamestown and Pocahontas by Scott O'Dell. Boston: Houghton Mifflin, 1987. [I] The reader is transported from lavish seventeenth-century English castles to early settlements at Jamestown.

Stranded at Plimoth Plantation 1626 by Gary Bowen. New York: Harper-Collins, 1994. [I] Journal entries of a young boy are used to re-create the daily life of the Pilgrims at Plymouth. The young boy is an orphan indentured by an unscrupulous uncle.

Nonfiction Trade Books

The American Reader: Words That Moved a Nation by Diane Ravitch (editor). New York: HarperCollins, 1990. [MS] Chronologically arranged, the book includes essays, speeches, poems, and songs about America from the 1600s to present. This annotated collection is an invaluable classroom resource.

Braving the New World, 1619–1784: From the Arrival of the Enslaved Africans to the End of the American Revolution by Don Nardo. Washington, DC: Chelsea, 1994. [I] This volume in the Milestones in Black American History series contains statistics on the number of slaves bought and traded, period art, photographs, and illustrations. Nardo vividly describes the growth of African slavery during the colonial era and the brutality on slave ships and plantations.

Eating the Plates: A Pilgrim Book of Food and Manners by Lucille Recht Penner. New York: Macmillan, 1992. [I] Details the eating habits, customs, and manners of the Pilgrims. The book is an interesting piece of social history.

Governing and Teaching: A Sourcebook on Colonial America by Carter Smith (editor). Highland Park, NJ: Millbrook, 1992. [MS] Historical, political, and religious aspects of life in colonial America are described and illustrated. This book is in the American Albums from the Collection of the Library of Congress.

Huskings, Quiltings, and Barn Raisings: Work-Play Parties in Early America by Victoria Sherrow, illustrated by Laura Loturco. New York: Walker, 1992. The author uses primary source material to tell how early Americans worked and socialized as they helped each other build houses, raise barns, clear land, harvest, and more. Sherrow ends the book with work-play activities in modern America.

If You Were There in 1776 by Barbara Brenner. New York: Bradbury, 1994. [I] People and events of the New and Old worlds at the time of the Revolutionary War are described. Brenner's major focus is on work, dress, home life, and recreation in the American colonies.

Junipero Serra by Sean Dolan. New York: Chelsea House, 1991. [MS] This book in the Hispanics of Achievement series tells the story of Father Serra, who left Spain to come to the New World as a missionary. When Jesuits were expelled from Spanish territory, he was assigned to California and founded a number of missions, including San Diego and San Francisco.

The Limits of Independence: American Women, 1760–1800 by Marylynn Salmon. New York: Oxford, 1994. [MS] Black-and-white photographs are included in this book in the Young Oxford History of Women in the United States series. The author uses numerous primary sources to provide information about the lives of women of different classes and cultures in colonial America.

Mason and Dixon's Line of Fire by Judith St. George. New York: 1991. [MS] St. George provides a history of the Mason-Dixon line from the 1730s to the 1880s. Charles Mason and Jeremiah Dixon, the French and Indian wars, the Whiskey Rebellion, Gettysburg, and more are found in this fascinating book.

Meet the Real Pilgrims: Everyday Life on Plimoth Plantation in 1627 by Robert H. Loeb. New York: Doubleday, 1979. [I] View the Pilgrims' homes, work, and surroundings through text, photographs, and line drawings. Lives and living conditions of the Pilgrims in early New England are well captured.

The Remarkable Voyages of Captain Cook by Rhoda Blumberg. New York: Bradbury, 1991. [I/MS] This exciting book reads like a novel as readers join Captain James Cook and his crews on his three voyages throughout the Pacific. The book includes many reproductions of paintings by artists who were on board.

Slave Ship: The Story of the Henrietta Marie by George Sullivan. New York: Cobblehill, 1994. [I] The author recounts a history of the slave trade and the discovery of the sunken slave ship the *Henrietta Marie*. He describes the recovery of the artifacts from the ship and the dedication of an underwater monument at the site.

Express Knowledge

1. Research, plan, prepare, and eat a meal that would have been typical of one in the colonial era.

2. Investigate songs that were sung during colonial times. Share your findings with your classmates.

3. Make a map of the thirteen colonies. Include major towns, rivers, and roads.

4. Imagine that you are a colonist. Write a letter to someone you left behind in your old country.

5. Make a diagram of a typical New England colonial settlement.

6. Read a book about the colonial period with at least one other person who is also interested in the period. As you are reading, frequently discuss chapters of the book.

7. Write a script for a play, skit, or readers' theater in which colonial leaders talk with one another about life during this period.

8. Make a list of major points of the Mayflower Compact. Give a speech to the class incorporating those major points.

9. Make a chart listing the thirteen colonies and include in your chart the founders of each colony, the reasons for the formation of the colony, type of government, and major characteristics of the colony.

10. Imagine you were an immigrant to North America during the 1600s or 1700s. Select your country of origin, age, gender, family circumstances, occupation, education, wealth, and talents. Write a short story about yourself as you might imagine your life.

11. Research some of the ways that colonists became informed about life outside of their communities. Illustrate the ways in which people received the news of their day and compare with today's communication.

12. Investigate how the colonists learned to grow crops and produce things for export.

13. Study the games that children played during colonial times. Learn how to play the games and develop a demonstration for classmates.

14. Make a poster showing some of the "blue laws" associated with the Sabbath.

15. Learn about the ancient folk beliefs of many colonists that resulted in the Salem witchcraft trials and belief in the so-called evil powers of some women. Make a presentation on the persecution of some women during the 1600s.

16. Study some of the contagious diseases that were a serious problem for colonists during colonial times. Make a chart showing the different diseases and common illnesses. Tell about colonial remedies and if cures were discovered.

17. Investigate early American furniture. Determine if it has made an impact on furniture today. Give specific examples.

18. Research the punishments that were handed down to people who committed crimes. How do they compare with punishments of today? Write your findings and take a position on whether any of the forms of punishment should be reinstated.

19. Investigate early public education. Develop a report that compares the education of today with education during colonial times.

Select Topic: Independence in 1783 to End of Civil War in 1865

The first government of the United States was formed in 1781; however, the Articles of Confederation that created the new government also caused many problems. By 1787, people in the new country felt that the government was a failure and that it was too weak to run the nation in an effective way. Thus, in 1787, representatives from each state met in Philadelphia to discuss the problems with the Articles of Confederation and soon realized that they had to write a new Constitution. The Constitution divides the powers of government between the federal government and the states. The federal government itself is also divided between the legislative, judicial, and executive branches. Importantly, the writers of the Constitution included a way to change the Constitution through amendments. Indeed, three years after the Constitution was ratified, ten amendments were added that are known as the Bill of Rights. The Bill of Rights protects individual rights and freedoms from the power of government.

George Washington became the first president of the United States in 1789. The District of Columbia was chosen as the nation's capital. The federal government survived some very difficult times in those early years.

When the third president of the United States, Thomas Jefferson, was in office, the United States doubled its size with the Louisiana Purchase from France in 1803. In addition to the vast land acquired from France, the United States acquired other territories as well, including Florida, Oregon, and the Southwest. Millions of people settled in the western states. Many were immigrants from other countries who were looking for a better way of life. Tremendous changes occurred during this time period, including the Civil War; however, we do not address the Civil War in this section because it is in Chapter 2.

Make Lists and Web

What We Want to Know

- Who was the first president?
- What were the Articles of Confederation?
- How did the thirteen new states get along with one another?
- Why did the leaders write a completely new Constitution?
- What is the Bill of Rights?
- Why and how was the Louisiana Territory explored?
- What happened during the War of 1812?
- Why did the United States declare war on Mexico?

- How did the pioneers go to the Far West?
- What happened to the Native Americans?
- How did early ways of travel differ from newer ways, such as the railroads?
- Why did the South secede from the Union?
- What was the Industrial Revolution?

Subtopics on the United States from 1783 to 1865

- Constitution and the Bill of Rights
- Purchase and exploration of the Louisiana Territory
- New territories acquired by the United States (Treaty of Paris, Spanish cession, Texas annexation, Mexican cession, Oregon country)
- Settlement of the West
- Forms of transportation

Form Study Committees and Develop Questions

Questions on the Constitution and the Bill of Rights

- Why did the Constitution replace the Articles of Confederation?
- Why did the Constitution provide for two houses of Congress?
- What made the delegates at the Constitutional Convention divide the government into three parts?
- Why were certain powers given to the states?
- How does the Constitution make changes possible?
- What is the Bill of Rights?
- What other changes have been made to the Constitution?

Study Topic

Fiction Trade Books

Beyond the Divide by Kathryn Lasky. New York: Dell, 1983. [I/MS] Meribah and her father, who was shunned by the Amish community, join the 1849 Gold Rush. Details in this survival novel are based on journals of the period.

Bold Journey: West with Lewis and Clark by Charlie Bohner. Boston: Houghton Mifflin, 1985. [I/MS] Young Hugh McNeal goes westward with the Lewis and Clark expedition in this novel of historical fiction. This chapter of history is turned into a real and believable adventure.

Bound for Oregon by Jean Van Leeuwen, illustrated by James Watling. New York: Dial, 1994. [I] The characters seem very real in this fictionalized account of nine-year-old Mary Ellen Todd's 1852 trip on the Oregon Trail. One event that makes this family's trek different from most other travelers' is an attack by Indians.

Christmas in the Big House, Christmas in the Quarters by Patricia C. McKissack and Frederick L. McKissack, illustrated by John Thompson. New York: Scholastic, 1994. [I] Preparations are being made to celebrate Christmas, the last Yuletide before the beginning of the Civil War. Amidst the gaiety, what are they talking about in the plantation house, the Big House? What were the slaves whispering among themselves in the Quarters?

A Gathering of Days: A New England Girl's Journal by Joan W. Blos. New York: Scribner, 1979. [I/MS] This Newbery Award winner brings the past to life. Readers can identify with fourteen-year-old Katherine, a New Hampshire farm girl, as she reveals an eventful time in her life through her journal.

Grandma Essie's Covered Wagon by David Williams, illustrated by Wiktor Sadowski. New York: Knopf, 1993. [I] The author's grandmother told him stories about the family's migration from Missouri to Kansas to Oklahoma looking for a better life. Williams writes of Grandma Essie's adventures.

Hugh Glass, Mountain Man by Robert M. McClung. New York: Morrow, 1990. [I] Written as fiction, this biographical novel is based on historical accounts of an early nineteenth-century fur trapper and explorer. Glass, who was mauled by a grizzly bear and left for dead, survived and dragged himself nearly two hundred miles across the frontier.

Underground Man by Milton Meltzer. San Diego: Harcourt, 1990. [MS] This thought-provoking novel geographically describes the antislavery movement and is based on the life of an actual nineteenth-century White abolitionist. Nineteen-year-old Josh becomes a conductor on the Underground Railroad and is tried and imprisoned.

Nonfiction Trade Books
The Bill of Rights: How We Got It and What It Means by Milton Meltzer. New York: HarperCollins, 1990. [MS] Clearly traces the history of the Bill of Rights. Includes the meaning of each of the ten amendments and contemporary interpretations of certain rights, such as gun control and censorship.

Cadets at War: The True Story of Teenage Heroism at the Battle of New Market by Susan Provost Beller. Cincinnati: Shoe Tree, 1991. [I] Describes participation of cadets from the Virginia Military Institute in an 1864 Civil War battle. Photographs as well as excerpts from diaries and letters are included.

Eli Whitney by Judith Alter. New York: Watts, 1990. [I] In addition to inventing the cotton gin, Whitney had other great achievements. Alter tells about his life and contributions.

George Washington and the Birth of Our Nation by Milton Meltzer. New York: Watts, 1986. [I/MS] This biography contains journal excerpts, drawings, and primary source material. Also included are Washington's notes for a draft of the United States Constitution.

Harriet Beecher Stowe and the Beecher Preachers by Jean Fritz. New York: Putnam, 1994. [I] Stowe's desire to convince people of the evils of slavery no doubt derived from the influence of her famous preacher father. In this lively biography, we learn that Harriet's father preferred sons since they could be raised to be preachers, but Harriet made her contributions in other ways.

Lewis and Clark: Explorers of the American West by Steven Kroll, illustrated by Richard Williams. New York: Holiday, 1994. [I] The journey of the Corps of Discovery is described. In addition to illustrations of the landscape, Williams painted portraits of expedition members and some of the Native Americans they met along the way.

Mary Lincoln's Dressmaker: Elizabeth Keckley's Remarkable Rise from Slave to White House by Becky Rutberg. New York: Walker, 1995. [MS] Elizabeth Keckley, a slave until her clients loaned her money to buy her freedom, was much more than a dressmaker to Mary Todd Lincoln. Rutberg pairs information from Keckley's autobiography with information on our country's history to give insight into the life of a slave before and after freedom and into the triumphs and tragedies of the Lincolns.

Shh! We're Writing the Constitution by Jean Fritz, illustrated by Tomie de Paola. New York: Putnam, 1987. [I] A beginning history of the Constitutional Convention. Amusing and based on careful research.

Express Knowledge

1. Write a paper about the Constitution that deals with several ideas. You may want to include the following: division of power, states that quickly approved the Constitution and why, and states that did not quickly approve the Constitution and why.

2. Pretend that you are George Washington and make a persuasive speech about the Constitution and the future of the United States. If possible, wear a wig and dress like him when you give your speech.

3. Make a chart showing the relationship between the Congress and the presidency. Include in the chart the length of term for senators, representatives, and the president; minimum age required; and citizenship requirements.

4. Make maps of the United States to show different ideas such as the following: the original thirteen colonies; the Louisiana Purchase; Spanish cession of Florida; Texas annexation; Mexican cession; and the Oregon Territory.

5. Read aloud to the class parts of *Poor Richard's Almanac* by Benjamin Franklin or parts of other books by Franklin.

6. Study the national anthem. Discuss who wrote it and why it is our national anthem, and examine the words and phrases of the song.

7. Pretend that you are Lewis or Clark and write a diary for the trip you make as you explore the Louisiana Territory. In your entries, include what you notice about Native Americans, animals, plants, rivers, land forms, and weather.

8. Make a poster that shows transportation during this time period, including canal boats, steamboats, stagecoaches, horses, and railroads. Also, show how transportation has evolved through history.

9. Make an illustrated timeline for the years 1783–1865 and mark the major events that occurred during that time.

10. Dramatize a scene from the "Trail of Tears." Consider preparing scripts for the dramatization of other scenes from this historical period. If you are working alone you could give a speech pretending you are Frederick Douglass at an abolitionist meeting.

11. Find copies of the *McGuffey Readers*. Compare the stories and other contents with textbooks that are used today.

12. Draw maps that chart the sequence of the frontier movement.

13. Design routes that are different from those used for the westward expansion into North America. Draw the routes and state why you believe they could have been used to travel west.

14. Identify the major reasons for the westward expansion into North America. Make a chart illustrating your reasons.

15. Compare the views of the abolitionists and of those who favored slavery.

16. Discuss how tariffs raised taxes and discouraged foreign competition during the early 1800s. Move the discussion to the present time and talk about whether the issues have changed or if they are the same.

17. Think about why George Washington opposed political parties. Develop a speech or a report about whether political parties are a good idea. Imagine what the United States would be like if Washington's advice had been followed.

18. Compare taxation in the United States following the Revolutionary War with today. Make a chart that compares the taxes then with the taxes your family pays both directly to the government and indirectly when they make purchases.

19. Research farming, transportation, and communication of the early 1800s and compare your findings with the technology of today. Consider making before-and-after sketches.

20. Develop a speech on the topic "The Rights of the American Indian." Document the national treatment of the American Indian and include as many injustices as you can uncover.

21. Conduct a debate about the establishment of the Electoral College and representation in the Senate and House of Representatives. Each side of the debate should focus on the views of large states such as Virginia and small states such as Rhode Island. Interview adults in the school, home, and community to see if the argument between large and small states still exists today.

22. Investigate the spoils system that was established in 1828. Discuss with a friend the fairness or unfairness of the system.

Select Topic: 1865 to 1914

In the years after the Civil War, the United States became an industrial nation. Machines were used to produce great quantities of goods and services. Manufacturing, coupled with a fertile agricultural land farmed with newly developed machinery, propelled the population growth and wealth of the nation.

People in other nations saw the United States as a land of opportunity. Thus, there were huge waves of European immigration to the United States during this time period.

Make Lists and Web

What We Want to Know
- What was the South like immediately after the war?
- What happened to African Americans in the South after the war?
- What laws were enacted to protect African Americans after the war?
- What impact did the completion of the transcontinental railroad have on the western and Great Plains states?
- What happened to the Native Americans?
- How were the Great Plains settled?
- Why did so many immigrants come to the United States?
- Why was there a tremendous growth in business and industry?
- What enabled the labor unions to become so powerful?
- Why was the Panama Canal built?

Subtopics on the United States from 1865 to 1914

- Immigration
- Reconstruction in the South
- Civil rights and segregation
- Railroads
- Settlement of the Great Plains
- Native Americans
- Growth of business and industry
- Labor unions

Form Study Committees and Develop Questions

Questions on Immigration

- Why did so many immigrants settle in the cities?
- What impact did the Homestead Act have on immigrants settling in the Great Plains?
- Why did millions of immigrants from Europe come to the United States?
- What were the immigration laws? Why?
- What was the role of Ellis Island as an immigration center?

Study Topic

Fiction Trade Books

The Barn by Avi. New York: Orchard/Jackson, 1994. [I] An Oregon Trail survival novel. Ben is sure that if he and his older siblings can finish building the barn, they will save their father who has suffered a stroke.

Beautiful Land: A Story of the Oklahoma Land Rush by Nancy Antle. New York: Viking, 1994. [I] On April 22, 1889, Annie Mae and her family are lined up with hundreds of other settlers to rush across the line and claim land in the Oklahoma Territory. This brief fictional account of a dramatic moment in American history is well told, although the author does not mention the disastrous effect on the Native Americans.

The Cat Who Escaped from Steerage: A Bubbemeiser by Evelyn Wilde Mayerson. New York: Morrow, 1990. [I] This short historical novel is a Jewish family's retelling of steamship passage from their native Poland to America. Reveals how families of all origins experienced steerage and life at sea.

From Sea to Shining Sea by Amy L. Cohn (editor). New York: Scholastic, 1993. [I] Contains stories, songs, essays, and poems related to all periods of American history. Illustrated by Caldecott Medal and Caldecott Honor Book artists.

The Long Journey of Lucas B. by Willi Fahrmann; translated from the German by Anthea Bell. New York: Bradbury, 1985. [MS] A fourteen-year-old journeys to America with a crew of carpenters hoping to find his father and earn money to take back to his family in a Prussian village. This translated text gives an interesting and unusual perspective on emigration in the 1870s.

Lyddie by Katherine Paterson. New York: Lodestar, 1991. [MS] In order to pay her family's debt, Lyddie Worthen leaves home to work in the factories of Lowell, Massachusetts. This book is rich in historical detail and vividly describes the daily lives of young girls who worked in the mills.

My Antonia by Willa Cather. Boston: Houghton Mifflin, 1962. [MS] The author provides a vivid picture of the strength and passion of a pioneer woman. Through the story of Antonia, the reader can visualize the lives of early pioneers.

The Other Shore by Lucinda Mays. New York: Atheneum, 1979. [MS] Learn about the lives of immigrants who worked in the sweat shops in New York City in the early 1900s. This novel is about a girl from Italy who immigrated to America with her family in 1911, and is told through flashbacks of her life in Italy.

Pioneer Cat by William Hooks. New York: Random House, 1988. [I] Nine-year-old Kate is traveling from Missouri to Oregon by wagon train and has hidden Scruggs, a cat, in her wagon. Kate cannot bear to give up Scruggs, even though pets are not allowed on the wagon train.

Prairie Songs by Pam Conrad, illustrated by Darryl S. Zudeck. New York: Harper, 1985. [I/MS] Set in late nineteenth–early twentieth-century Nebraska, this story reveals the beauty and harshness of pioneer life. The frail young wife of a doctor is unable to adapt to the hardships of pioneer life.

Sarah, Plain and Tall by Patricia MacLachlan. New York: Harper, 1985. [I] This touching story of life on the early U.S. frontier deserves its prize-winning status. Will Sarah, who answered a newspaper ad for a wife, find the prairie as appealing as her sea in Maine?

Winding Valley Farm: Annie's Story by Anne Pellowski. New York: Philomel, 1982. [I] This novel is based on the lives of the author's ancestors. Pellowski chronicles everyday happenings of a Polish American family on a Wisconsin farm in the early 1900s.

Nonfiction Trade Books

Across America on an Emigrant Train by Jim Murphy. New York: Clarion, 1993. [I] Many of Robert Louis Stevenson's own words are used as the author describes the young writer's journey from Scotland to California to see the woman he loved. Murphy includes experiences of other emigrants on the train trip across America and some history of the building of the transcontinental railroad.

Annie Oakley and the World of Her Time by Clifford Lindsey Alderman. New York: Macmillan, 1979. [I] Accurate historical information is presented in this book about Annie Oakley. This fascinating story tells how the independent young sharpshooter made history.

Bully for You, Teddy Roosevelt by Jean Fritz. New York: Putnam, 1991. [I/MS] Fritz truly captures the energetic personality of Teddy Roosevelt, our twenty-sixth president. The times and the man come alive through interesting anecdotes.

Children of the Wild West by Russell Freedman. New York: Clarion, 1983. [I/MS] Authentic photographs complement this readable text dealing with the westward movement. Different aspects of life in the American West from 1840 to the early 1900s are presented.

The Chinese Americans by Milton Meltzer. New York: Crowell, 1980. [MS] Tells of the struggles and contributions of Chinese immigrants to America. Period photographs illustrate the story.

Coming to America: Immigrants from Southern Europe by Gladys Nedler. New York: Delacorte, 1982. [MS] The histories of people from Italy, Greece, Portugal, and Spain are portrayed. The book addresses a part of the mass immigration between 1880 and 1930.

Cowboys of the Wild West by Russell Freedman. New York: Clarion, 1985. [I/MS] The late-nineteenth-century decades of the cowboy are portrayed in this fascinating text. The photographs and fine writing make this a must to learn about the romance of the Old West and the historical realities of cattle ranching.

Crazy Horse by Judith St. George. New York: Putnam, 1994. [I] Crazy Horse died in 1877, only a year after defeating Custer at the Battle of the Little Bighorn. St. George uses numerous oral history records and writings for this informed account of the life and leadership of Crazy Horse.

Dorothea Lange by Robyn Montana Turner. New York: Little, Brown, 1994. [I] This excellent biography is a tribute to Lange, a pioneer in the area of documentary photography. Included in the book are some powerful photographs of American life, such as *White Angel Breadline* and *Migrant Mother*.

Eight Hands Round: A Patchwork Alphabet by Ann Whitford Paul, illustrated by Jeanette Winter. New York: HarperCollins, 1991. [I] This book is a history lesson told through the alphabet. Each illustrated patchwork pattern is accompanied by a history of its origin.

The Factories by Leonard Everett Fisher. New York: Holiday, 1979. [I/MS] The human side of the first textile mill in New England and the 1876 Exposition is presented through anecdotes. Fisher's scratchwood illustrations enhance this book, which is good for both reading and research.

From Slave to Civil War Hero: The Life and Times of Robert Smalls by Michael L. Cooper. New York: Lodestar, 1994. [I] During his seventy-six years, Smalls rose from a slave to a free man and on to political leader. The struggles of Reconstruction, some events of the Civil War, and the social climate during the period of slavery are woven into the story of Robert Smalls.

Frontier Home by Raymond Bial. Boston: Houghton Mifflin, 1993. [I/MS] Through photographs and text, Bial provides an inside look at the daily life of early settlers. Includes interior and exterior close-ups of a frontier home.

Gold Rush: The Yukon Stampede by Margaret Poynter. New York: Atheneum, 1979. [I/MS] Photographs and maps illustrate this book, which tells about the lives of those willing to gamble everything they owned to seek gold in the northlands. The book takes place during the depression of 1896, when gold was discovered in the Yukon River Valley.

I Was Dreaming to Come to America selected and illustrated by Veronica Lawlor. New York: Viking, 1995. [I/MS] Part of the Ellis Island Oral History Project, this book includes the recollections of fifteen immigrants who passed through Ellis Island between 1900 and 1925. Lawlor's hand-painted collages reflect the imagery of the memories of these immigrants.

Johnny Appleseed by Reeve Lindbergh. New York: Joy Street, 1990. [I] This biographical poem is a glorious celebration of the life of John Chapman. Better known as Johnny Appleseed, this missionary and naturalist took apple trees and seeds to settlers of the American frontier.

The Little House Cookbook: Frontier Foods from Laura Ingalls Wilder's Classic Stories by Barbara M. Walter, illustrated by Garth Williams. New York: Harper, 1979. [I] This book presents more than one hundred pioneer recipes. The anecdotes and historical information also make for interesting reading.

Lonesome Whistle: The Story of the First Transcontinental Railroad by Dee Brown. New York: Holt, 1980. [MS] This book is the story of the building of the first transcontinental line in the 1860s. It tells about the plans to build the railroad and about the immigrants who did the actual work.

Mr. Marley's Main Street Confectionery by John J. Loeper. New York: Atheneum, 1979. [I/MS] Visit an old-time candy shop through this fascinating account of how sweets came to America. The history of candy, sundaes, Cracker Jack, and other sweet treats is discussed.

Mother Jones and the March of the Mill Children by Penny Colman. Highland Park, NJ: Millbrook, 1994. [I] This biography of Mary Harris "Mother" Jones focuses on the 1903 protest march she organized to defend the rights of underage mill workers. Her fight for the end of child labor is well illustrated with photographs and drawings.

Pioneer Children of Appalachia by Joan Anderson, photographs by George Ancona. New York: Clarion, 1986. [I] Photographed at the living-history museum in Fort New Salem, West Virginia, this photo essay reveals the life of an extended family of nineteenth-century settlers of Appalachia.

Prairie Visions: The Life and Times of Solomon Butcher by Pam Conrad. New York: HarperCollins, 1991. [I] Solomon Butcher migrated to Nebraska in 1880, where he collected true stories and took photographs of prairie families. Conrad presents an intriguing and dramatic account of the photographer and of prairie life.

The Price of Free Land by Treva Adams Straight. Philadelphia: Lippincott, 1979. [I] Homesteading in western Nebraska comes alive as the author recounts her family's pioneer experiences beginning when she was five years old. The book is illustrated with photographs from the family album.

Reconstruction: America After the Civil War by Zak Mettger. New York: Lodestar, 1994. [MS] This unsettled period of American history is well portrayed through accounts of individuals and archival photographs and drawings. Both advancement and persecution of newly freed African Americans are given attention in this book from the Young Readers' History of the Civil War series.

Express Knowledge

1. Write newspaper articles that might have appeared in Southern and Northern newspapers immediately following the Civil War.

2. Make a circle graph depicting information such as the following: employment in major industries in different years; population in different regions of the country; population in rural areas and urban areas; and the number of immigrants from different countries at different points in time.

3. Construct models of different types of housing, such as frame houses, log cabins, sod houses, and adobe houses.

4. Make an illustrated timeline of major events from 1865 to 1914.

5. Make a chart that shows important inventions. Include the year each was invented and the name of the inventor.

6. Write excerpts from selected books and post them on the bulletin board. These books, for example, could be biographies or autobi-

ographies of famous people during this time period or could be works of fiction.

7. Trace the history of your family and make a family tree. You might find that your ancestors immigrated to America during this period of time. Share your family trees with one another by displaying them in the classroom.

8. Pretend you are living in a selected era and write a letter to the president of the United States expressing your views about current issues of the time. For example, write to President Theodore Roosevelt expressing your views about the construction of the Panama Canal.

9. Write a short biography of one of the leaders in this time period, such as William Jennings Bryan, William McKinley, Theodore Roosevelt, Frederick Douglass, or Lucy Stone.

10. Create a class book of poems or songs that were written within the time frame of this TI.

11. Make a graph of the wholesale price index from 1865 to 1914.

12. Copy an article from a current magazine or newspaper that discusses a current problem in farming, industry, economy, equality, or labor unions. Compare and contrast it with a problem from 1865 to 1914.

13. Form a study group to read and discuss the lives of women leaders, such as Susan B. Anthony and Florence Kelley, in the early women's movement for equality.

14. Build models of the different apparatuses used to transport people and various items out West.

15. Collect clippings from old and current newspapers and magazines about the settlement of your country or state.

16. Compose the lyrics for a song that a new settler in the United States might have sung.

17. Criticize the manner in which natural resources were destroyed in the settlement of the United States. Make an oral or written report stating your criticisms.

18. Dramatize the feelings of a new immigrant arriving at Ellis Island in the early 1900s.

19. Summarize the settlement pattern of one immigrant group, such as the Swedes or Irish (or your own ancestors if they came from Europe or Asia), after they came to the United States.

20. Draw a map of the United States and mark the ports of entry for immigrants.

21. Study the craft of quilting and replicate designs on paper or by making quilt squares. Collections of quilt squares can be sewn together to form a wall hanging or a quilt.

Resources
Professional Books for Teachers

The following books have been selected to support you as you deepen your knowledge about settling the United States and to assist you in developing your curriculum. Some books may contain information you can share with students by reading aloud or sharing sections of the book.

CALIFORNIA DEPARTMENT OF EDUCATION. 1991a. *American Indian: Yesterday, Today, & Tomorrow*. Sacramento: California Department of Education.

————. 1991b. *United States History and Geography: Making a New Nation*. Sacramento: California Department of Education.

COMMAGER, HENRY, AND MILTON CANTOR. 1988. *Documents of American History, Vol. 1: to 1898*. Englewood Cliffs, NJ: Prentice-Hall.

HOPKINS, LEE BENNETT, COMP. 1994. *Hand in Hand: An American History Through Poetry*. New York: Simon and Schuster.

PELZ, RUTH. 1990. *Black Heroes of the Wild West*. Seattle: Open Hand Publishing.

PFEIFFINGER, CARLA R. 1991. *Social Studies Readers for Children*. Englewood, CO: Teachers Idea Press.

PHILIP, NEIL. 1995. *Singing America: Poems That Define a Nation*. New York: Viking.

RAVITCH, DIANE. 1990. *The American Reader*. New York: HarperCollins.

Reader's Digest. 1978. *American Folklore and Legend*. New York: Reader's Digest Association.

SCOTT, JOHN A., ed. 1991. *Living Documents in American History*. New York: Washington Square Press.

WERNER, EMMY E. 1995. *Pioneer Children on the Journey West*. New York: HarperCollins.

Westward Expansion: Exploration & Settlement: Perspectives on History. 1991. Carlisle, MA: Discovery Enterprises.

Wigginton, Eliot, ed. 1972. *The Foxfire Book: Hog Dressing, Log Cabin Building, Mountain Crafts, Food Planting by the Signs, Snake Lore, Hunting Tales, Faith Healing, Moonshining and Other Affairs of Plain Living*. New York: Doubleday.

Documents

Many primary source materials are available so students can see a copy of the original document, and read the actual text or see photographs and prints of an event. The following list represents some places to find primary sources. Many of the addresses are in the list at the end of this chapter or the list in Appendix A.

- Congressional Research Service, Library of Congress
  Information packs on many historical topics (contact member of Congress from local district)

- Government Printing Office
  Presidential speeches

- Historical Societies (state and local)
  Early reports, historical writing, reproductions and photographic collections, speeches, messages, treaties, records of conventions, correspondence, land records, census reports, and much more

- Knowledge Unlimited, Inc.
  Explorer maps, including the Oregon Trail, and posters related to settlement

- Libraries (state and local)
  United States Statutes at Large, *Congressional Records* for each Congress of the United States, congressional committee reports, volumes of presidential papers for each president, court case volumes, and much more

- Library of Congress, Documents Superintendent
  Route maps of explorers

- Library of Congress, National Archives
  Reproductions of historical map collection

- National Gallery of Art
  Color reproductions of American artists' works

- National Register Information System
  Lists produced according to location, historical function, historical theme, and other categories

- United States Corps of Engineers, Army Map Service
  Railroad maps of the United States

Selected Print

There are so many different series available that it is impossible to list all of them. We have included several that we would use in TIs.

- *Cobblestone: The History Magazine*
  Many issues devoted to United States settlement themes, such as Jamestown and "Aftermath of the Civil War: Reconstruction"

- Colonial Williamsburg
  Toll-free number for information (1-800-HISTORY)

- Children's Press
  A series titled Cornerstones of Freedom, which includes *The Women Who Shaped the West*

- Digest Books
  A replica of an early Sears catalog, *Sears, Roebuck & Co. 1908 Catalogue No.* 117

- Greenhaven Press, Inc.
  Several series of materials include: Opposing Viewpoints Junior series; *Christopher Columbus*, The Way People Live series; *Cowboys in the Old West*, World History series; *The Relocation of the American Indian, American Frontier*, and *The Lewis and Clark Expedition*

- Pleasant Company Publications
  American Girls Collection includes series on Colonial America, Pioneer America, Civil War America, and America's New Century and character dolls, maps showing where the girls lived, cookbooks for the period, and costumes from the period

- Scholastic Company
  Children of the Wild West series, including . . . *If You Traveled West in a Covered Wagon*

- Sundance Publishing Company
  Perspectives on History includes many primary and secondary source materials; Connect Social Studies Era Units and Era Libraries include *The Revolutionary War* and *The Civil War*

- Teaching with Historic Places
  Plans for teaching about many places, including *The Liberty Bell: From Obscurity to Icon*; *The Ohio and Erie Canal: Catalyst of Economic Development for Ohio*; *Chattanooga, Tennessee: Train Town*; *Memories of Montpelier: Home of James and Dolley Madison*

Media

Many wonderful videotapes, audio recordings, maps, posters, and other materials are available from a variety of resources. We have listed a few that we have examined, but many more exist.

- Coronet
  English and Dutch Colonization in the New World

- Finley-Holiday
  Where America Began: Colonial Williamsburg, Jamestown, Yorktown

- Golden Owl
  Kits in U.S. *History Source Collection*, including "Salem Village & Witch Hysteria" and "Immigration During Colonial Times"

- History Channel on many local cable stations
  Weekly programming for recording of historical documentaries

- Public Broadcasting Service
  Catalogs listing documentary series and individual videos

- Recorded Books, Inc.
  Audiotaped books including *Caddie Woodlawn* (Carol Ryrie Brink),

On to Oregon! (Honore Morrow), *Mr. Revere and I* (Robert Lawson), *Mr. Tucket* (Gary Paulsen)

- Smithsonian Books/Recordings/Videos
  Many different resources available for purchase from Smithsonian collection

- Smithsonian/Folkways Recordings, Center for Folklife Programs and Cultural Studies
  Over 2,100 historic recordings available on audiocassette

- SSSS (Social Science School Service)
  Videos from the SSSS catalog include: *Mayflower Voyagers*; *My Mother, the Witch*; *Pilgrim Journey*; *The Americas, 1996*; *Virginia Plantations: Mount Vernon, Monticello, and Other Great Houses of Old Virginia*; *Building of the Transcontinental Railroad*; *Lewis and Clark at the Great Divide*; *Music and Heroes of America*; *Frontier Experience*; and *Opening the West*

- WEM Records
  Moving West: Songs with Historical Narration and *Colonial and Revolutionary Songs* by Keith and Rusty McNeil

Technology

Use of the computer expands each day; therefore, it is impossible to list current individual programs and World Wide Web sites.

- World Wide Web sites
  Interviews and photographs on historical settlement of the United States

- Internet/e-mail
  Correspondence with others interested in a specific topic about settlement of the United States

- CD-ROM programs
  American Heritage Illustrated Encyclopedia Dictionary. Xiphias, 1993. (Includes thousands of American history vocabulary words with graphics.)

  Archives of History: A Moving-Image of the 20th Century. MPI Multimedia, 1993. (Includes video clips of many events dating back to 1896.)

  Landmark Documents in American History. Facts on File, Department Alfa-Informatica, University of Groningen, 1995.

  Smithsonian's America. Creative Media, 1994. (Includes artifacts, documents, photos, posters, and video segments that document American history and culture.)

People

Almost every community has individuals who are knowledgeable on a TI topic. As you know, they can be found near the school (parents, staff members, and community members), in private and public agencies, and at local universities and colleges. We have listed some of the people we would invite to speak to our students.

- Museum officials and historical society staff
- Librarians
- Representatives of Native American tribes/bands
- College and university faculty members
- History society/club members
- Older family members
- Elderly residents, including those in retirement and nursing homes
- Quilters (demonstrate process and different patterns and share examples)
- Other knowledgeable community members

Interview Question Ideas

The following interview questions are meant to be a beginning point as your students develop questions of their own.

Interview Questions About Settling the United States

- Do you remember any stories that were told by relatives about living conditions when they moved to the United States? If Native American, do you remember any stories that have been told about when European settlers came to North America?

- Do you remember or know any stories about the kinds of homes your ancestors had?

- What kind of food did you eat when you were little? Do you remember any stories by older relatives about when they were little?

- What kind of work did family members engage in, and how many years did they devote to that work?

- What historical events did members of your family live through? Are these relatives alive so they can tell their story or do you remember what they told you?

- Did you or any family members live through a terrible tornado, earthquake, flood, drought, or epidemic?

- Do you remember any of the details of the disaster?

- Did any of your family help to settle any place in the United States? Do you know any stories that have been passed down? Are there any written records?

- Do you remember any celebrations that followed World Wars I or II, Korea or Vietnam?

- What were members of your family doing during any of the wars?

Family History

Family and oral history interviews are very similar in the way they are conducted. We have listed them separately but we encourage you to refer to the information in both sections. Refer to Appendix E for additional information on conducting family history interviews.

The members of many families moved westward across the United States. If family members have been in the United States for a long time, they may have witnessed or been a part of many historical events. Too often people are overlooked who made a great contribution to the history of the United States by doing the kind of labor that wasn't rewarded with big salaries or schools named in their honor.

Oral History

Oral history ideas are included that can be photocopied and given to students to serve as a springboard for the development of their questions. Because oral and family history projects have similarities, we encourage you to read the family history section. Refer to Appendix E for additional information on conducting oral history research.

Oral history projects about the settling of the United States offer an understanding of history that cannot be found in books. Older citizens can share their memories of events from the past. *Foxfire*, compiled by the students of Eliot Wigginton, is an excellent example of documenting history in rural Georgia. There are many other examples of oral history projects throughout the United States. Your local historical society or library may have on file some examples of oral histories that have been compiled in your community.

Begin an oral history project by using some of the following ideas:

- Settlement of your community: Inquire about historical events that took place during the settling of the United States in your local community. When did the earliest settlers come to the area? Where did they come from? What were the specifics of the settlement?

- Natural disasters: Talk to older community members or read old newspapers to identify natural disasters that have occurred since the settlement of your community. When did each disaster happen? What was the extent of the damage? Did anyone die? How was the damage repaired?

- Big buildings: The central areas of many cities have one or more large buildings. Who built the building? When was it built? What was the purpose of the building? How much did it cost? Where did the material come from? Who have been the owners of the building through the years?

- Big houses: Most towns have some large houses that evoke the curiosity of people who see them. Who built the house? When was it built? What was the owner's occupation? Where did the materials to build the house come from? How many different families have lived in the house?

- Scandals: Many towns have had a few scandals over the years since they were settled. Read old newspapers and talk to older residents about crimes that have been committed, such as arson, bank robberies, and kidnapping. Who did it? What were the circumstances? What happened at the trial? What punishment did anyone receive?

Transcription of the oral history interview and any available photographs should be placed in the school library and the historical society.

Field Trips

In many communities there are places that students can visit to gain a deeper understanding of a topic. This list of places are where we would want to take students during a TI. We suggest that in addition to planning class field trips, you also might develop a list of places where families could visit. The list could be sent home as part of a letter to parents (see Appendix D for parent letter ideas). Most local communities have places to visit that provide firsthand information about settlement of the United States. Provide lists of places for parents so they can plan family outings. Some places we recommend include:

- Historical societies
- Cemeteries (dates on tombstones, information on epidemics and ages at death)
- Libraries (exhibits and primary source documents)
- Courthouses (early records)
- Native American historical centers and tribal museums
- Historical landmarks
- Museums
- Historical houses/districts

- Historical reenactments
- History clubs' exhibits
- Political party headquarters
- Old churches and missions
- Archaeological excavations of early settlements
- Private collections of early documents and artifacts
- Living history museums (located in many states)

Art

There are several art forms unique to the United States that were developed during the settling of the country. Examples include quilting, crafts, early American furniture, and early paintings. Examples of these art forms can be viewed at museums, galleries, historical societies, and in private collections. Sets of reproductions of early American art, photograph collections, and slide collections are available from museums, historical societies, and galleries.

BALLINGER, J. 1989. *Frederic Remington*. New York: Harry N. Abrams Inc./National Museum of Art.

Creative Teaching Press. 1994. "Westward Expansion." Vol. V, *American Artists Reflect American History Series*. Cypress, CA: Creative Teaching Press.

Davis Publications. 1987. *Discover Art*. Worcester, MA: Davis Publications. (Grade five includes lessons in colonial portraiture and art of western America.)

EWENS, J. C. 1965. *Artists of the Old West*. New York: Doubleday.

National Museum of American Art. 1991. *The West as America*. Washington, DC: National Museum of American Art. (Lesson plans on nineteenth-century American artists.)

PIRTLE, C., and Texas Cowboy Artists Association. 1975. *The American Cowboy*. Birmingham, AL: Oxmoor House.

- New York Graphic Society
  Large and small study prints and posters by many early American artists. Other prints can be ordered from the following places:

    Amon Carter Museum of Western Art, P.O. Box 2365, Fort Worth, TX 76113

    The Fine Arts Museum of San Francisco, San Francisco, CA 94118

    The Metropolitan Museum of Art, 255 Gracie Station, New York, NY 10028

    National Gallery of Art Reproductions and Publications, Publications Service, Washington, DC 20565

    Philadelphia Museum of Art, Benjamin Franklin Parkway, Box 7646, Philadelphia, PA 19101

The St. Louis Art Museum, Museum Shop, Forest Park, St. Louis, MO 63110

The Taft Museum, 316 Pike Street, Cincinnati, OH 45402

Thomas Gilcrease Institute of American History and Art, 1400 North 25th West Avenue, Tulsa, OK 74127

- Six early artists who have many available works include Samuel Seymour, George Catlin, Karl Bodmer, Frederic Remington, Nathaniel Currier, and James Ives.
- The Sutlery Inc., National Cowboy Hall of Fame, 1700 Northeast 63rd, Oklahoma City, OK 73111
- Quilting is an American art form. Books with quilting designs can be found in libraries and craft stores. Many areas of the country have groups of quilters who enjoy sharing their art with students.

Music

Many songs that children enjoy have been written about the settlement of the United States. "The Erie Canal" remains a favorite, along with hundreds more.

Four important musical forms developed during the settlement of the United States: spirituals, blues, jazz (including ragtime), and bluegrass music. Spirituals were songs developed by African American slaves. Each song had special significance and was often an expression of religious feelings or a description of the hardships in the slaves' lives. Bluegrass music is an original musical form from Appalachia which was developed in the 1900s using string instruments.

The Smithsonian has a large collection of music recordings, including a good deal of folk music that tells about the settling of the United States. Song collections include:

ARNETT, H. 1975. *I Hear America Singing! Great Folk Songs from the Revolution to Rock.* New York: Praeger.

DALLIN, L., AND L. DALLIN, COLLECTORS. 1980. *Heritage Songster.* Dubuque, IA: William C. Brown.

FIFE, A. E., AND A. S. FIFE. 1969. *Cowboys and Western Songs: A Comprehensive Anthology.* New York: Clarkson N. Potter.

FOX, D., ed., with C. MARKS. 1987. *Go In and Out the Window: An Illustrated Songbook for Young People.* New York: Henry Holt.

METROPOLITAN MUSEUM OF ART WITH BUFFALO BILL HISTORICAL CENTER. 1991. *Songs of the Wild West.* New York: Simon and Schuster.

MUNK, B. 1993. "Songs of Pioneer Mid-America." Vol. 1, *Our Heritage of American Folk Songs.*

SCOFIELD, T. 1981. *An American Sampler.* Eugene, OR: Cutthroat Press.

SCOTT, J. A. 1983. *The Ballad of America: The History of the United States in Song and Story.* Carbondale: Southern Illinois University Press.

SEEGER, P. 1961. *American Favorite Ballads: Turns and Songs as Sung by Pete Seeger.* London: Oak Publication.

SILBER, I., EDITOR. 1967. *Songs of the Great American West.* New York: Macmillan.

Addresses

The addresses in this section are provided because each is a source of information or materials related to TIs on the settling of the United States. Other addresses can be found in Appendix A. (Please check the *Encyclopedia of Associations* found at many public libraries for the most current addresses.)

National Register of Historic Places, Interagency Resources Division, National Park Service, U.S. Department of the Interior, P.O. Box 37127, Washington, DC 20013-7127

National Trust for Historic Preservation, 1785 Massachusetts Avenue, N.W., Washington, DC 20036

U.S. Government Printing Office, Superintendent of Documents, Washington, DC 20402

Global Awareness

4

Global awareness helps students move from an ethnocentric perspective to a broad-minded view of the world. As students view the world through "global eyes," they realize we are all a part of the human family; they learn to respect and value people of different cultures and nationalities as well as their own rich heritage.

Through global education, students learn and understand how to cope with the interdependent world and to resolve problems of the world. It is desirable for students to make lifelong personal commitments to participate responsibly by using their abilities to promote peace for humanity and ecology on our planet.

Students learn skills that help them cooperate and compete with individuals in other nations; these skills facilitate their understanding of a variety of international and intercultural issues and of the relationships between global issues and local concerns.

In this section, we provide three different TIs on global awareness: (1) Interdependence and World Peace; (2) United Nations as Peacekeeper; and (3) Nations of the World.

Select Topic: Interdependence and World Peace

We are experiencing an accelerating growth of interdependence between people of different cultures, civilizations, and regions in numerous ways, such as technology, politics, and economics. It is important that we cooperate and compete with individuals in other nations and understand a variety of international and intercultural issues and the relationships between global issues and local concerns.

We are all members of the human race on this earth, and we must respect one another. We must strive to make peace in the world a reality. We must develop appropriate ways to use our intelligence and creativity to develop new tools to peacefully resolve disagreements between nations.

Make Lists and Web

If you and your students have selected this topic, the next step is to assess your students' prior knowledge by asking them to tell what they know about interdependence and world peace. We suggest a whole-class brainstorming session in which you make a list of what they know on a transparency or on the chalkboard. After this list is completed, encourage the class to ask questions about what they would like to know. The following may help you and your students as you make your own lists of "What we want to know."

What We Want to Know

- What has caused the increase in global interdependence?
- How have multinational corporations (MNCs) affected interdependence among nations?
- Why do nations restrict trade? What are the results of such restrictions?
- In what ways are we interdependent?
- Why is a global culture developing?
- Why is Western influence throughout the world decreasing?
- What are the effects of the globalization of America?
- What is the relationship between global issues and local concerns?
- How does our worldview compare with worldviews held by individuals in other nations?
- How do globalization and decreasing American influence affect America's relationship with other countries?
- What is the relationship among rising population growth, standards of living, and environmental problems in the world?
- How do narrow nationalism, dogmatic ideologies, and an endangered environment affect chances of worldwide peace?
- How can we have security in a nuclear age?
- What can be done about the gap between rich and poor nations?
- How does resource depletion affect the peoples of the world?
- What can be done about the deterioration of the ecosphere?
- What are similarities and differences between people of different nations?

After the class has thought about what they want to know and the questions are formulated, it is time to organize the study. Ask the students to review all of their questions in order to develop a list of subtopics that represent the questions. Remind them that one question often relates to more than one subtopic. In the large group, guide students to generate a list. The following list of subtopics on interdependence and world peace might give you ideas as you and your students make your own list.

Subtopics on Interdependence and World Peace

- Peace in the world
- Ways we are interdependent: economics, ecology, politics, technology, and medicine
- International law
- Effects of narrow nationalism
- Standards of living throughout the world
- Global issues and local concerns
- Worldwide women's issues
- Universal human rights
- Nuclear proliferation
- Effects of globalization on America and other nations
- Causes of globalization
- Causes of international conflicts

A list of subtopics has been decided and now a web can be made. Web the major subtopics that you and the students have identified and then add subordinate ideas to the subtopics. You will probably web on the chalkboard or overhead and then copy the final web on paper so that students can later refer to it.

Form Study Committees

After completing a web, the students should be organized into study committees. You and the students need to decide with whom students will work in their small groups and what topics they prefer to research. If you have a group of twenty-four students, for example, you might form six groups of four students in each group. In this case, you might limit the number of subtopics to six, with each group studying one of the subtopics.

Develop Questions

Students must be interested enough in a topic to raise questions and to explore those questions through research. Ask each group to develop as many questions as they can think of and then record them on a blank transparency so they can share them with the rest of the class and hear their comments.

If you have a study committee on peace in the world (the first subtopic listed), the students might develop some of the following questions, or you might suggest that they research some of these questions.

Peace in the World

- How do we work toward peace in the world?
- What are some causes of conflict?
- How can conflict between nations be resolved peacefully?
- How does peace in the world at this time compare with peace during other periods of time?
- How can better international understanding contribute to peace?
- What are ways that we can increase international understanding?
- How do nuclear arsenals affect peace?
- Why is it more important than ever that we seek peace between nations?

Study Topic

Once students have identified questions relevant to their topic, they begin the study. As students engage in study, they add questions and delete some of their original ones. They use many resources, including books, nonprint sources, magazines, newspapers, and computers.

Fiction Trade Books

The Big Book for Peace by Ann Durell and Marilyn Sachs (editors). New York: Dutton, 1990. [I/MS] Thirty-four well-known authors and illustrators look at peace, conflict, war, and resolution through original illustrated stories and poems. Readers will find new perspectives and ways of thinking about peace as they read these different points of view.

Peace Tales: World Folktales to Talk About by Margaret Read MacDonald. New Haven, CT: Linnet, 1992. [I/MS] Collection of folktales from different cultures around the world reflecting aspects of war and peace. They can be used as springboards for discussing issues of peace and cooperation.

Nonfiction Trade Books

Elie Wiesel by Caroline Lazo. New York: Dillon, 1994. [MS] In this book in the Peacemaker series, Lazo combines photographs and Wiesel's own words to tell his life story. The review of his life includes the horrific experiences in Nazi camps that led to his lifetime of fighting oppression.

Journey to the Soviet Union by Samantha Smith. Boston: Little, Brown, 1985. [I] Samantha dedicated this book "to the children of the world.

They know that peace is possible." Yuri Andropov, then general secretary of the Central Committee of the Communist Party of the USSR, invited Samantha to visit the Soviet Union. Wonderful photographs accompany this text in which Samantha details her trip and her visit to the international children's camp, ARTEK.

Neve Shalom/Wahat al-Salam by Laurie Dolphin, photographs by Ben Dolphin. New York: Scholastic, 1993. [I/MS] This photo-essay reveals the friendship of two ten-year-old boys in a school where half of the students are Arab and half are Jewish. The reader is introduced to the work of the Oasis of Peace School.

On the Wings of Peace: Writers and Illustrators Speak Out for Peace; In Memory of Hiroshima and Nagasaki by Sheila Hamanaka. New York: Clarion, 1995. [I/MS] This tribute to survivors of war and to peacemakers includes stories, poems, and beautiful artwork contributed by more than sixty noted writers and artists. At the end of the book are directions for folding a paper crane and an extensive biography of peace resources.

Peace and Bread: The Story of Jane Addams by Stephanie McPherson. Minneapolis: Carolrhoda, 1993. [I/MS] Nobel Peace Prize recipient Jane Addams worked among the poor in Chicago and had leadership roles in international organizations for world peace. The author focuses on Addams's career, but also includes some information on her early years.

Peace Begins with You by Katherine Scholes, illustrated by Robert Ingpen. San Francisco: Sierra Club, 1993. [I] Scholes talks about the concepts of peace, conflict, resolution, and how to be a peacemaker. Appealing multiethnic illustrations complement the text.

The Peace Commandos: Nonviolent Heroes in the Struggle Against War and Injustice by Michael Kronenwetter. New York: New Discovery, 1994. [MS] A book in the Timestop series that presents a survey of pacifism. The author concentrates on American history with an emphasis on wars during the twentieth century, but does mention some famous names in the field, such as Gandhi and Dorothy Day.

The Peace Seekers: The Nobel Prize by Nathan Aaseng. Minneapolis: Lerner, 1987. [I/MS] Aaseng tells the stories of eight Nobel Peace Prize recipients, including Jane Addams, Martin Luther King, Jr., Lech Walesa, and Andrei Sakharov.

People of Peace by Rose Blue and Corinne J. Naden. Brookfield, CT: Millbrook, 1994. [I] Five Americans and eight Nobel Peace Prize winners are included in this book, which profiles eleven individuals who have brought about positive change. The authors present the successes of these peace advocates and also tell of failed efforts.

Rigoberta Menchu by Caroline Lazo. New York: Dillon, 1994. [I] Rigoberta Menchu, who won a Nobel Peace Prize for her struggles for the rights of indigenous peoples in Guatemala, is little known in the United States. This biography, in the Peacemaker series, is clearly written and illustrated with black-and-white photographs.

Samantha Smith: A Journey for Peace by Anne Galicich. Morristown, NJ: Silver Burdett, 1987. [I/MS] Describes Samantha Smith's trip to the Soviet Union at the invitation of Yuri Andropov and her travels and speeches to promote peace and understanding. Galicich tells about the deaths of Samantha and her father, and her mother's current work.

Talking Peace: A Vision for the Next Generation by Jimmy Carter. New York: Dutton, 1993. [MS] Carter tells of his personal work in promoting peace and discusses how young people can "wage peace." He analyzes the causes and effects of conflict and explains the need for nonviolent resolution.

Women of Peace: Nobel Peace Prize Winners by Anne Schraff. Springfield, NY: Enslow, 1994. [MS] Part of the Collective Biographies series, this book describes the lives of eight women who have been awarded the Nobel Peace Prize. The biographical sketches are enhanced with information about the political and social conditions that inspired the women to work for peace and justice.

Express Knowledge

1. Find factual information on peace. Make a short presentation about world peace at a parent-teacher meeting or at a public event.

2. Prepare a display on peace in a mall or at a public event such as a weekend art show. You might distribute leaflets on promoting peace. (Before making arrangements, find out the rules for displaying and check to make certain that you have adult supervision for the activity.)

3. Make a list of organizations that promote peace in the world and distribute the list in the community.

4. Develop a public service announcement on world peace for a local television or radio station. Contact the stations before you begin to ask about the specifications for such announcements (length, format, style). If the announcement is scheduled to air, inform classes in the school to listen.

5. Write a poem about peace and then share the poem with others by reading it aloud or publishing it in a class book.

6. Make a list of things in your home that were grown or made in another country; list the country of origin for each item.

7. Make a list of items that are grown or made in the United States and the countries to which the items are exported.

8. Make a list of items that are grown or made in your local community and the countries to which they are exported.

9. Investigate symbols that represent peace. Design your original peace symbol and combine the symbols in a display.

10. Collect fiction and nonfiction books about peace and develop an exhibit that can travel around the school.

11. Make a chart displaying the costs of different wars in terms of the loss of lives, military expenditures, and environmental damage.

12. Interview relatives and friends concerning their views about war and peace. Chart the results of your interviews.

13. Organize a youth summit on peace by inviting interested students from other classrooms to discuss world peace issues. Make news organizations aware of your summit.

14. Conduct a computer search on nuclear proliferation. Record the total number of entries and then list selected international meetings, articles, films, or recordings and other titles.

15. Select one major problem in the world, such as human rights violations, hunger, environmental concerns, or infectious diseases. Read a wide variety of newspapers and magazines and collect articles on the topic for a one-week period. Make a bulletin board with the results of your research. Include a summary of your views as you take a stand on the issue.

16. Write a letter to local and state newspapers stating your views on deforestation and desertification in the world. Ask other classes to sign the letter to show wide support for your ideas.

17. Draw a map of the world and color all the countries in which over 50 percent of the people are below the poverty level. At the bottom of the map, list some of the poorer countries and write their national debt and gross national product (GNP).

18. Write a Human Rights Declaration for the world. Ask other students and adults to contribute ideas to the declaration. Consider the possibility of your classroom or school adopting the declaration. Ask the local newspaper to print it.

19. Study the life of Jane Addams, the social worker from Chicago. Who are the modern-day Jane Addamses and what contributions are they making to the world? Make a poster telling about the lives of some of these women and men.

Select Topic: United Nations as Peacekeeper

The United Nations was formed before the end of World War II. Representatives of fifty-one nations met in San Francisco and signed an agreement on April 25, 1945, for the formation of the United Nations. The United States and the other member nations agreed to work for peace through the United Nations.

Make Lists and Web

What We Want to Know

- When and why was the United Nations formed?
- What are the goals of the United Nations?
- Why is the headquarters of the United Nations in the United States?
- How many countries belong to the United Nations?
- What actions can the United Nations take if a country is not acting responsibly?
- What are some of the accomplishments and failures of the United Nations?
- Why are international inspections of nuclear power facilities important?
- What are reasons why some Americans do not like the United Nations?
- How is the United Nations organized?
- In addition to peace, what are some other concerns of the United Nations?

Subtopics on the United Nations

- Accomplishments and actions of the United Nations
- Formation of the United Nations
- Goals of the United Nations
- Organization of the United Nations
- Concerns of the United Nations (environment, health, human rights, international development, peace, and security)

Form Study Committees and Develop Questions

Accomplishments and Actions of the United Nations

- What have been some major accomplishments of the United Nations?

- How have these accomplishments affected world peace?
- What have been some major actions of the United Nations?
- How have these actions affected the lives of people in the world?
- How have people in the world viewed the actions of the United States?
- What are some areas in which the United Nations has not been able to achieve success? Why?
- How can the United Nations be made more effective?

Study Topic

Fiction Trade Books

The Whispering Cloth by Pegi Deitz Shea, illustrated by Anita Riggio. Honesdale, PA: Boyds Mills Press, 1995. [I] The illustrations and text of this picture book capture the life of refugees, the Hmongs from Laos, who live in Ban Vinai, a camp in Thailand. The story unfolds as Mai, her mother and grandmother embroider story cloths to sell to traders. (The camp is similar to the many refugee camps supervised by agencies of the United Nations.)

Nonfiction Trade Books

A Brave and Startling Truth by Maya Angelou. New York: Random House, 1995. [I/MS] A poem written and read by Angelou for the fiftieth anniversary of the founding of the United Nations, celebrated in San Francisco in 1995.

The Future of the United Nations by Raymond Carroll. New York: Watts, 1995. [MS] Examines the origin, history, accomplishments, and weaknesses of the United Nations. Carroll describes the effects of the veto rule in the Security Council and discusses criticism of the United Nations' effectiveness.

Search for Peace: The Story of the United Nations by William Jay Jacobs. New York: Scribner, 1994. [I] Discusses the history, organization, and special agencies of the United Nations. The 1948 Universal Declaration of Human Rights and a timeline are included.

The United Nations by Stewart Ross. New York: Bookwright Press, 1990. [MS] Describes the League of Nations and the goals and organization of the United Nations. Includes its history, structure, seven case studies of United Nations involvement, and problems of concern.

The United Nations by R. Conrad Stein. Chicago: Children's Press, 1994. [I] A book in the Cornerstones of Freedom series. The author tells why the United Nations was created, describes its composition and its operations, and evaluates its impact.

The United Nations by Adams Woog. San Diego: Lucent, 1993. [MS] A book in the Overview series. Includes primary sources and discusses organization, current roles, and future issues of the United Nations.

United Nations—Peacekeeper? by Edward James Johnson. New York: Thomson Learning, 1995. [I/MS] Examines the peacekeeping missions of the United Nations since its beginning. Includes maps, glossary, "fact files," photos, and relevant newspaper clippings.

Where the River Runs: A Portrait of a Refugee Family by Nancy Price Graff. New York: Little, Brown, 1993. [I/MS] The book describes each of three generations of a Cambodian refugee family now living in Boston. Discusses the aspirations and problems of recent immigrants, many of whom have been assisted by a United Nations agency.

A World in Our Hands: In Honor of the 50th Anniversary of the United Nations by Young People of the World Staff. Berkeley, CA: Tricycle Press, 1995. [MS] Children wrote, illustrated, and edited this book in celebration of the fiftieth anniversary of the United Nations. A foreword by Secretary General Boutros Boutros-Ghali tells about the work of the United Nations and offers a challenge for readers to be better global citizens.

Express Knowledge

1. Make a chart detailing the functions of the United Nations.
2. Set up a mock United Nations Security Council meeting to debate or deliberate issues concerning UN involvement in a part of the world where there is a war or threat of a war.
3. Write a history of the United Nations beginning with the League of Nations.
4. Write a report or make a presentation on one of the special agencies of the United Nations:World Health Organization (WHO); International Labor Organization (ILO); International Monetary Fund (IMF); World Meteorological Organization (WMO); International Bank for Reconstruction Development (World Bank); Food and Agricultural Organization (FAO); and UN Educational, Scientific, and Cultural Organization (UNESCO).
5. Investigate different countries that do not belong to the United Nations. Make an oral report about how many countries do not belong and cite possible reasons.
6. Identify the reasons why some United States citizens don't want their country to belong to the United Nations. List the reasons on a chart.
7. Read the Universal Declaration of Human Rights that was approved by the United Nations in 1948. Imagine what the world

would be like if the document were fully realized around the world. Prepare a presentation in which you share your ideas.

8. Outline some of the accomplishments of the United Nations. Place the outline on a chart.

9. Investigate the work of UNICEF (United Nations Children's Fund) and find out if any community members help raise money for the fund. Share what you have learned with classmates and ask them to consider sponsoring a project.

10. Find examples of worldwide conferences sponsored by the United Nations to raise the awareness of human rights issues around the world.

11. Summarize some of the environmental concerns of the United Nations. Analyze the reasons why not all the world's governments are voluntarily reducing pollution and protecting their natural resources.

12. Conduct a survey of family and community members by asking questions about their perceptions of the value, the accomplishments, and the potential of the United Nations.

Select Topic: Nations of the World

It is important that we understand the perspectives of people in other nations because we will develop a greater appreciation for them. We can learn from international scholars in many disciplines as we enhance our own knowledge in the social sciences, mathematics, science, business, industry, and the arts. Our respect for other people in the world will also increase as we compare our own values and beliefs with those of people in other nations.

Make Lists and Web

What We Want to Know

- Where is the nation located?
- How do people dress?
- What type of climate exists in the country?
- What kinds of food do people eat? Have eating habits changed in recent years? If so, why?
- What kinds of homes do people have?
- How are children educated?
- What is the popular music of the country?
- What types of art are typical of the country?

- What religions do the people practice?
- What games do children play?
- What languages do they speak?
- What is interesting about the country's history?
- What kind of government does the country have?
- What is the economic condition of the country? What trade agreements does it have with other countries?
- What is its population? Is it increasing or is it stabilizing? Why?
- What is happening to the environment in the country?
- What kinds of agricultural products are produced in the country?
- What is manufactured in the country?
- What minerals and natural resources are available in the country?

Subtopics on Nations of the World

- Economic conditions
- Agriculture
- Arts and literature
- Clothing
- Environment
- Foods
- Form of government
- History of the country
- Housing
- Geographic location
- Climate
- Industry and agriculture
- Language(s) spoken
- Population growth
- Religions
- Transportation

Form Study Committees and Develop Questions

Questions on Economic Conditions

- How does the weather affect the country's economy?
- What are the leading products of the country? Why?
- What are major exports and imports? Why? Who are the country's major trading partners? Why?

- How has the economy changed in the past fifty years?
- How has military conflict affected the country's economy?
- How has the government affected the nation's economy?

Study Topic

Fiction Trade Books

Among the Volcanoes by Omar S. Castaneda. New York: Lodestar, 1991. [I/MS] Isabel Pacay, a young Mayan peasant, wants to become a teacher but must give up her dream and accept home responsibilities. Provides insight into life in a contemporary Guatemalan village.

Chopsticks from America by Elaine Hosozawa-Nagano, illustrated by Masayuki Miyata. Chicago: Polychrome Publication Corporation, 1994. [I] A story about two children, nine and five, born of American parents. They move back to Japan and discover that life in the country of their forebears isn't what they expected, but they learn to be tolerant and accepting of the differences.

Crocodile Burning by Michael Williams. New York: Lodestar, 1992. [MS] Sowetan teenager Seraki Nzule is able to forget all his troubles and the violence and oppression of South Africa when he joins a township musical group. Only after the group returns home from performing in New York does he decide to do something positive with his life.

Dear Mr. Sprouts by Errol Broome. New York: Knopf, 1993. [I] Freddie lives on a farm in Australia and one day discovers a balloon with a packet of seeds and a letter from a girl named Inke. Readers learn about Freddie and Inke and their growing friendship through the letters they write each other.

Do You Know Me by Nancy Farmer, illustrated by Shelley Jackson. New York: Orchard, 1993. [I] The reader sees the contrast between traditional living in the bush and modern life in the city in this novel set in Zimbabwe. Topiwa's uncle from the country comes to live with her family in the city and the two get into interesting situations—especially with their money-making schemes.

The Ear, the Eye and the Arm by Nancy Farmer. New York: Orchard, 1995. [MS] Follow Tendai, Rita, and their little brother Kuda as they explore their perilous city in Africa and are tracked by detectives with folkloric talents. An imaginative fantasy set in Harare, Zimbabwe, in 2194.

The Future-Telling Lady and Other Stories by James Berry. HarperCollins, 1993. [I] Berry gives insight into life in the West Indies in these six original stories. The stories range in subject matter and go from realistic to fantastic.

Grab Hands and Run by Frances Temple. New York: Orchard, 1993. [MS] After Felipe's father's motorbike is found abandoned outside the city, the family knows they must leave El Salvador. Felipe, his sister, and his mother travel through Guatemala and Mexico and into the United States in this very exciting and heartbreaking novel.

The Ink-Keeper's Apprentice by Allen Say. Boston: Houghton Mifflin, 1994. [MS] In this autobiographical novel set in postwar Japan, Say tells the story of a teenager's apprenticeship to a master cartoonist. Fans of Say's picture books will be happy to read about the young artist.

Is Underground by Joan Aiken. New York: Delacorte, 1993. [I] In this book in Aiken's Wolves Chronicles series, Is travels to London to look for her lost cousin, Arun, only to find the city half empty of children. She learns they have been lured away to Playland and, of course, clever Is is able to rescue the lost children.

Jacob's Rescue: A Holocaust Story by Malka and Michael Halperin. New York: Bantam Skylark, 1993. [I] When eight-year-old Marissa's father and uncle were children they lived in Warsaw and were hidden by a special couple during the Holocaust. Marissa hears the story of their experiences during her family's traditional Passover seder in Israel.

My Brother, My Sister, and I by Yoko Kawashima Watkins. New York: Bradbury, 1994. [I/MS] This story is a continuation of the book *So Far from the Bamboo Grove*. It is an autobiographical account of the author and her sister, who have been reunited with their brother, and of the many hardships they face as they struggle to survive in postwar Japan.

Sky Legends of Vietnam by Lynette Dyer. New York: HarperCollins, 1993. [I] As the title implies, this is a collection of Vietnamese stories explaining celestial phenomena. It includes elements of culture and a pronunciation guide to Vietnamese names.

So Far from the Bamboo Grove by Yoko Kawashima Watkins. New York: Lothrop, 1986. [MS] Eleven-year-old Yoko tells about her family and their forced departure from North Korea at the end of World War II. This autobiographical novel is both horrifying and touching.

Thames Doesn't Rhyme with James by Paula Danzinger. New York: Putnam, 1994. [I] In this sequel to *Remember Me to Harold Square*, Kendra gets to see her long-distance boyfriend when her family spends the Christmas holidays in London. Readers will get a fun perspective on British culture as they join the city scavenger hunt planned by the adults.

Tonight by Sea by Frances Temple. New York: Orchard, 1995. [I/MS] Set in a tiny community in Haiti, this compelling novel tells of hardships faced by a proud and resourceful people. The book is action-packed and well written.

Where the Flame Trees Bloom by Alma Flor Ada, illustrated by Antonio Martorell. New York: Atheneum, 1994. [I] The author reminisces about her childhood in rural Cuba in these eleven short stories. Readers will feel as though they have been there and have met the memorable characters.

The Year of Impossible Goodbyes by Sook Nyull Choi. Boston: Houghton Mifflin, 1991. [I/MS] Ten-year-old Sookan tells the story of her family's experiences in North Korea during the Japanese occupation at the end of World War II and then the Russian occupation. This autobiographical novel is a heartbreaking story of suffering, love, and determination.

Nonfiction Trade Books

Amazon by Peter Lourie, photographs by Marcos Santilli. Honesdale, PA: Boyds Mills Press, Inc., 1991. [I] A modern-day account of the life of the people in the Brazilian state of Rôndonia in the Amazon, which is often described as the world's last frontier. The photographs make the life of the people in this great rain forest come alive.

Bedouin by John King. Chatham, NJ: Raintree-Steck, 1993. [I] Children will be fascinated by this account of the nomadic Bedouins' way of life in this book in the Threatened Cultures series. The Bedouins, whose culture is being threatened for a number of reasons, live in various countries of North Africa and the Middle East.

Behind the Border by Nina Kossman. New York: Lothrop, 1994. [I] The author describes her childhood in Soviet Russia during the 1960s. She provides autobiographical vignettes of her life at school and home.

Children Just Like Me by Susan Elizabeth Copsey with Anabel Kindersley (compilers). New York: Dorling-Kindersley, 1995. [I/MS] The vivid photography of Barnabas Kindersley brings alive this book about children of different cultures. The book introduces the lives and aspirations of children around the world.

China by Pamela Tan. New York: Cavendish, 1993. [MS] This excellent book in the Women in Society series provides information on the changing roles of women in Communist China. Included are photographs and profiles of outstanding women and their contributions.

Days of the Dead by Kathryn Lasky; photographs by Christopher C. Knight. New York: Hyperion, 1994. [I] A Mexican family honors their ancestors as they prepare for and celebrate the Days of the Dead holiday. Food preparation and the cemetery ceremonies are depicted.

Door of No Return: The Legend of Goree Island by Steven Barboza. New York: Cobblehill, 1994. [I] For five centuries Africans were captured and shipped away in bondage from Goree Island, off the coast of Senegal. Barboza recounts the history of the island and tells about present-day life in Goree.

Hopscotch Around the World by Mary D. Lankford, illustrated by Karen Milone. New York: Morrow, 1992. [I] Children around the world play different varieties of hopscotch. Each page in the book contains a hopscotch diagram.

India by Vijaya Ghose. New York: Cavendish, 1994. [MS] This book in the Women in Society series looks at the economic, political, religious, and cultural norms that affect the status of women in India.

Jerusalem Mosaic: Young Voices from the Holy City by I. E. Mozeson and Lois Stavsky. New York: Four Winds, 1994. [I/MS] Jewish, Muslim, and Christian teenagers tell about their lives in the volatile city of Jerusalem. They share their dreams, fears, and thoughts about family and community relationships.

My Place by Nadia Wheatley, illustrated by Conna Rawlins. La Jolla, CA: Kane/Miller, 1992. [I] This fascinating book uses child narrators to tell about a single tract of land, "my place," over a two-hundred-year span. The book moves backward every ten years from 1988 to 1788, describing lifestyles of the families and changes in the land.

Over Here It's Different: Carolina's Story by Mildred Leinweber Dawson. New York: Macmillan, 1993. [I/MS] An eleven-year-old girl from the Dominican Republic compares life in America with that in her native country. Many photographs by George Ancona accompany the story.

The Riddle of the Rosetta Stone: Key to Ancient Egypt by James Cross Giblin. New York: HarperCollins, 1990. [I/MS] The secrets of ancient Egypt are unlocked in this fine piece of nonfiction. Translating the Rosetta Stone is treated as a mystery with clues in Greek, demotic writing, and hieroglyphics.

Showa: The Age of Hirohito by Dorothy Hoobler. New York: Walker, 1990. [MS] Provides a look at Japanese history during the reign of Emperor Hirohito (1926–1989). Focuses on the emperor himself, but gives insight into the social, political, economic, and moral issues of his time.

SovieTrek: A Journey by Bicycle Across Russia by Dan Buettner. Minneapolis: Lerner, 1994. [I] Two Americans and two Russians travel seven thousand miles across southern Russia by bicycle. Meet the people and learn about their customs in this entertaining travelogue.

Talking Walls by Margy Burns Knight, illustrated by Anne Sibley O'Brien. New York: Tilbury House, 1992. [I] Knight introduces the reader to children of the world and its different cultures through walls ranging from the Lascaux Cave paintings to the recently destroyed Berlin Wall. The text is accompanied by a double-page spread illustration of each wall.

Uncertain Roads by Yake Strom. New York: Four Winds, 1993. [MS] This informative book documents the culture of the millions of Rom who live in Hungary, Romania, Sweden, and Ukraine. Strom tells about his travels and includes many statements from interviews with both teenagers and adults.

Express Knowledge

1. Draw a map of the world and color all the countries that have over 50 percent of the people below the poverty level the same color. At the bottom or top of the map, list some of the poorer countries and write their national debt and gross national product. Display the map in your classroom.

2. Make a graph showing the population of the country you are studying compared to the populations of ten other countries.

3. Write brief sketches of three famous people from the country you are studying.

4. Make an illustrated fact book of the country you are studying. List each fact and then give a brief description of it.

5. Identify a problem that confronts the country; after studying the problem, identify several possible solutions that you would suggest to the leaders of the country.

6. Write a paragraph in which you describe the economy of the country you are studying. In a second paragraph, describe the economy of the United States or the economy of another country.

7. Make a list of the major landforms of the country. You might want to show these landforms on a map of the country.

8. Write a report on one of the major religions of the country you are studying.

9. Make one of the handicrafts (goods made by hand) of the country you are studying.

10. Make a comparison chart that shows the similarities and differences between the country you are studying and another country.

11. Make and illustrate a timeline that shows major events that have occurred in the nation's history.

12. Draw and color the flag of the nation. If possible, write a brief description of the origin of the flag.

13. Research the national anthem of the country you are studying.

14. Write a newspaper article about an event in the country. Remember to tell who, what, when, where, why, and how. Study articles in the newspaper to help you write your own article.

15. Make a list of facts and opinions about the country. You might want to make a list of opinions that a citizen of the country might make and a list of opinions that a citizen of the United States or another country might make about the same topic.

16. Make a circle graph of the literacy rate (percentage of people who can read and write) of the country. Compare the percentage with those of other countries, including the United States.

17. Collect magazine and newspaper articles about the country you are studying. Put the clippings in a notebook or post them on a bulletin board.

18. Make a diagram showing the major sections of the government of the country.

19. Make a circle graph showing the percentage of imports to the country and another graph showing the percentage of exports from the country.

20. Make an oral report about one of the topics, issues, personalities, or sites related to the country you have studied.

21. Make a chart showing a major river in the country and compare it with several other major rivers of the world. You might include the following information: length, body of water it flows into, how people use the river, and the area drained.

22. Obtain travel posters of the country and post them in your room. If you cannot obtain any from a travel agency or another source, consider making your own.

23. Take an imaginary trip to the country and keep a journal of your travels. Make entries that tell several things, such as the following: location, sites, weather, customs, food, and the people. You might want to mention how the country differs from your own.

24. Pretend that you have just been elected leader of the country. Write your inaugural speech and then share it with your class.

25. Make an outline that traces the roots of conflict within the country or with another country. In addition, you might want to describe

how the conflict could have been prevented and how it could be resolved.

26. Write a report about a major philosopher in the country's history or present time. Tell how that person has influenced the development of the country.

27. Read aloud poetry from the country to your class.

28. Write poetry that is in the style of the poetry you are reading.

29. Describe in writing basic changes that have taken place in the country in the past one hundred years.

30. Make a picture dictionary of key vocabulary words important to the study of the country.

31. Prepare an oral report about an animal or plant you find particularly fascinating that lives in the country you are studying.

32. On a map, show the ten largest cities of the country. Indicate the population of each.

33. Interview someone who has visited the country you are studying. If possible, conduct the interview in your classroom so that your classmates can hear it.

34. Make a puzzle of the country, drawing the outlines of the divisions of the country, such as states or provinces. Label each division by name and with color. Now cut out the divisions along the borders. When finished, put the puzzle back together again and ask classmates to do the same.

35. Visit the grocery store and other types of stores. Make a list of the items you find that were produced in the country you are studying.

36. Prepare several true-false questions about the country you have been studying. Give the test to a friend to see if he/she can answer the questions.

37. Write a letter to a pen pal your age in the country you are studying (or write to a pretend pen pal). Tell about the things in your country that are similar and different. If you have e-mail capabilities in your classroom or school, try writing an actual letter to a pen pal in that country.

38. Produce a video or audiotape of a documentary program on the country you are studying. Include at least five topics in your documentary.

39. Use the Internet to appeal to a student from another country who is learning English to communicate with you. Tell the student about your life in the United States and ask the student to write to you and tell you about life in his/her country.

40. Look on the World Wide Web for pages completed by students in foreign countries to help readers appreciate the culture of the country. Analyze whether the information will help to dispel stereotypes and inaccurate beliefs about the country.

Resources
Professional Books for Teachers

The following books have been selected to provide support as you deepen your own knowledge about peace and the world and to assist you in developing your curriculum. Some books may contain information you can share with students by reading aloud or by sharing sections of the book.

BECKER, J. M. 1973. *Education for a Global Society*. Bloomington, IN: Phi Delta Kappa Educational Foundation.

BOULDING, E. 1988. *Building a Global Civic Culture*. New York: Teachers College Press.

FLETCHER, R. 1986. *Teaching Peace Skills for Living in a Global Society*. New York: Harper & Row.

FREIRE, P. 1973. *Pedagogy of the Oppressed*. New York: Seabury Press.

GRANT, J. 1994. *The State of the World's Children*. New York: Oxford Press/UNICEF.

HANVEY, R. G. 1987. *An Attainable Global Perspective*. New York: Global Perspectives in Education.

HEATER, D. 1984. *Peace Through Education: The Contribution of the Council for Education in World Citizenship*. London: Falmer Press.

HOFFMAN, D., D. SIMMONETT, AND M. SORENSON. 1991. *A Child's Right: A Safe and Secure World*. New York: United Nations.

MCKISSON, M., AND L. MACRAIE-CAMPBELL. 1990. *Our Divided World: Poverty, Hunger & Overpopulation*. Tucson: Zephyr Press.

NURKSE, D., AND K. CASTELLE. 1990. *In the Spirit of Peace: A Global Introduction to Children's Rights*. New York: Defense for Children International USA.

REARDON, B. 1988. *Education for Global Responsibility: Teacher-Designed Curricula for Peace Education, K–12*. New York: Teachers College Press.

ROCHA, R., AND R. OTAVIO. 1989. *The Universal Declaration of Human Rights, An Adaptation for Children*. Brazil: Salamandra Editorial/United Nations Publications.

STOMFAY-STITZ, A. M. 1993. *Peace Education in America*. Metuchen, NJ: Scarecrow Press.

TYE, K., ed. 1991. *Global Education: From Thought to Action*. Alexandria, VA: Association for Supervision and Curriculum Development.

UNICEF. 1991. *First Call for Children*. New York: UNICEF.

UNITED NATIONS. 1992. ABC: *Teaching Human Rights*. New York: United Nations.

————. 1994. *United Nations Day Program Manual*. New York: UNA-USA.

WALTER, V. 1993. *War and Peace Literature for Children and Young Adults: A Resource Guide to Significant Issues*. Phoenix: Oryx Press.

ZOLA, J. 1985. *Teaching About Peace and Nuclear War: A Balanced Approach*. Boulder, CO: Social Science Education Consortium.

Selected Print

There are so many different series available about countries in the world that it is impossible to list all of them. We have included several that we would use in TIs.

- *Breakthrough*
  A publication of Global Education Associates, 475 Riverside Drive, Suite 456, New York, NY 10115 (all issues focus on some aspect of education for a global future)

- *The Bridge*
  An international newspaper written for youth and published by Youth Ambassador, Dept. B, P.O. Box 5273, Bellingham, WA 98227 (accepts youths' contributions of stories, poems, pictures, and art)

- Carolrhoda
  World's Children series

- Cavendish
  These series from Cavendish provide useful and interesting information for TIs in this chapter: Cultures of the World; Women in Society

- Chelsea House Publishers
  Series of books titled American Women of Achievement that includes *Jane Addams*

- Dillon
  Discovering Our Heritage series; Global Villages series

- Greenhaven Press
  Series to foster social interaction between and among students, including Opposing Viewpoints Junior series (*Acid Rain*, *Forests*, *Nuclear Power*, *Pollution*, *Toxic Wastes*, *Poverty*, *Hunger*, *The Homeless*); Overview series (*Homeless Children*, *Illiteracy*, *World Hunger*); The Way People Live series (*Life on an Israeli Kibbutz*, *Life in an Eskimo Village*)

- HarperCollins
  Portraits of the Nations series

- The Lerner Group
  Series of books including The World's Children, The Suitcase Scholar, Visual Geography series, and Easy Menu Ethnic Cookbooks

- Peace Links, Women Against Nuclear War
Kits including Global Awareness, Reach for Peace, Talking to Your Children, and Celebrating Peace
- Smithsonian Resource Guide for Teachers
Lists many visual arts sources about African art and culture
- Teaching with Historic Places
Plans for teaching about the following places: *First Lady of the World: Eleanor Roosevelt at Val-Kill; Clara Barton's House: Home of the American Red Cross; Castolon: A Meeting Place of Two Cultures; Fort Hancock; Herbert Hoover: Iowa Farm Boy and World Humanitarian;* and *Thaw in the Cold War: Eisenhower and Khrushchev at Gettysburg*

Media

Many wonderful videotapes, audio recordings, maps, posters, and much more are available from a variety of resources. We have listed a few that we have examined, but many more exist.

- Recorded Books Inc.
Audiotape books include *Anne Frank: The Diary of a Young Girl* and *The Crossing*
- Knowledge Unlimited
Videocassettes and CD-ROMs on world cultures
- SSSS (Social Studies School Services)
Catalog lists many different media concerning global awareness

Technology

Since use of the computer expands each day, it is impossible to list current individual programs and World Wide Web sites about peace.

- World Wide Web sites
Information on countries, peace, and the United Nations
- Internet/e-mail
Correspond via e-mail with other students about peaceful solutions to world problems

  Computer programs:

- Broderbund Software, Inc., *Macglobe*, 1992
- MECC-Minn. Educational Computing Corporation (*Dataquest: Asia & Oceania, MECC Dataquest: World Community* [1987], *World Geography*)
- Tom Snyder Productions (PC *Globe, The Other Side* [1985])

People

Almost every community has individuals who are knowledgeable about the United Nations, other countries around the world, and people who work for world peace. As you know, they can be found near the school (parents, staff members, and community members), in private and public agencies, and at local universities and colleges. We have listed some of the people we would invite to speak to our students.

- Medical doctors or nurses who work in underdeveloped countries
- Furloughed or retired missionaries
- Local peace advocates
- Fund-raisers for UNICEF
- Travel agents who book trips/tours to foreign countries
- Parents and community members who have traveled to specific countries or regions
- Foreign students who attend local colleges or universities
- Recent immigrants
- Members of local ethnic organizations
- Locally recognized authorities from colleges and the community
- Representatives from embassies and consulates
- Peace Corps volunteers
- Former exchange students

Interview Question Ideas

The following interview questions are meant to be a beginning point as your students develop questions of their own.

Interview Questions for a New Immigrant

- Will you tell me about the country where you lived?
- Were you born there?
- How many years did you live there?
- How does that country differ from where you live now?
- Tell me about customs that are different from those here?
- What holidays do you celebrate that aren't celebrated in the United States?
- What do you miss? Why?
- Is there anything you like better in the United States?

Family History

Family and oral history research are very similar in the way they are conducted. We have listed them separately but we encourage you to refer to the information in both sections. Refer to Appendix E for additional information on conducting family history interviews.

Unless students are Native American, they have ancestors who immigrated to the United States from another country. If these ancestors are alive, they can possibly be interviewed. If they aren't alive, perhaps other family members have memories of or knowledge about the immigration.

Oral History

Oral history ideas are included that can serve as a springboard to other ideas. For information on oral history, refer to Appendix E.

Oral history research is similar to family history research except students view everyone in the community as a possible source of information. Most communities in the United States have residents who immigrated from another country. Conduct oral history to record the memories of these immigrants for future generations to read.

Field Trips

In most communities there are places where students can visit to help them develop a global perspective. We suggest sending home a list of possible field trip sites related to the TI because parents may want to visit them with their children.

- University international houses
- Local cultural clubs for people of different countries
- Performances of groups from foreign countries
- Museums for displays of art from other countries
- Art galleries for collections or exhibits of art from a specific country or region
- Import shop to study art forms
- Import food shops to find foods of the country or region

Fantasy Field Trip

Students can engage in a fantasy field trip. They can pretend to visit the country for a vacation or to become Peace Corps volunteers or UNICEF workers who visit villages in a third world country. They can pretend they are helping with health care, hunger relief, education, or the building of housing. The steps include:

1. Choose the country, the dates of the trip, and the amount of money you will spend per person.

2. Research the country by reading books, travel guides, and brochures.

3. Collect artifacts, pictures of people and sights, and maps.

4. Check on applying for passports and visa requirements. Secure an application form for a passport and make copies so everyone can fill out the form. If a visa is necessary, write to the embassy of the country and request a form.

5. Call airlines or travel agents to seek information about flight schedules to and ground transportation in the country. Pretend to book reservations for all travel.

6. Check travel guides for hotels and write pretend letters to make reservations.

7. Investigate the following: time zone changes to plan for jet lag, monetary units and exchange rates, credit card use, foods, purchase of traveler's checks, tipping customs, taxes applied to purchases and hotels, average temperatures and rainfall, clothing customs, emergency medical care, electrical current for appliances, holiday dates.

8. Plan a schedule for each day of your trip.

9. Pretend to go to the airport, fly and land in the country, clear immigration, and execute your travel plans. Pretend to fly back to the United States and clear U.S. customs and passport control. Think about your jet lag.

10. Evaluate your trip. Did you accomplish your goals? How much money did you spend? What would you do differently on your next trip?

Art

When studying the art of any culture or country, help students develop an understanding of and appreciation for the aesthetic contributions. Help them learn whether the art form is aesthetic, social, educational, political, religious, or a combination.

When viewing artifacts from another country, inquire if they are airport tourist art or authentic to the country.

Music

All countries have some form of music that is a unique part of the culture. Find recordings of music made by artists and musical groups from the country or continent. For example, when studying Africa, find musical instruments such as drums, recordings of tribal music, and pictures of instruments.

Pen Pal Sources

League of Friendship, Inc., P.O. Box 509, Mount Vernon, OH 43050-0509

Student Letter Exchange, R.R. 4, Box 109, Waseca, MN 56093

World Pen Pals, 190 Como Avenue, St. Paul, MN 55208

Addresses

The addresses in this section are provided because each is a source of information or materials related to a TI on peace. (Please check the *Encyclopedia of Associations* found at many public libraries for current addresses.) The embassies of most foreign countries are in Washington, DC. Addresses can generally be found in the reference section of a public library.

American Forum for Global Education (Global Perspectives in Education, Inc.), 45 John Street, Suite 1200, New York, NY 10038

Americans for Human Rights and Social Justice, P.O. Box 5258, Fort Worth, TX 76115

Amnesty International, 322 Eighth Avenue, New York, NY 10001

Anti-Defamation League, 823 United Nations Plaza, New York, NY 10017

Asia Society, 725 Park Avenue, New York, NY 10021

Beyond War Foundation, 222 High Street, Palo Alto, CA 94301

Carnegie Endowment for International Peace, 11 Dupont Circle, Washington, DC 20036

Center for Global Education, Augsburg College, 731 22nd Avenue South, Minneapolis, MN 55454

Committee on Foreign Affairs, U.S. House of Representatives, Washington, DC 20510

Council for a Livable World, 20 Park Plaza, Boston, MA 02116

Educators for Social Responsibility, 23 Garden Street, Cambridge, MA 02138

Food and Agriculture Organization of the United Nations, via delle Terme di Caracalla, 1-00100 Rome, Italy

Freedoms Foundation at Valley Forge, Valley Forge, PA 19481

Global Perspectives in Education, 219 East 18th Street, New York, NY 10003

Global Tomorrow Coalition, 1325 G Street, N.W., Suite 915, Washington, DC 20003

International Association of Educators for World Peace, P.O. Box 3282, Mastin Lake Station, Huntsville, AL 35810

International Friendship League, 40 Mount Vernon Street, Boston, MA 02108

Peace Corps, 1990 K Street, N.W., Washington, DC 20526

Stanford Program on International Cross-cultural Education, Lou Henry Hoover Building, Stanford University, Stanford, CA 94305

UNICEF, Program Publication, DH-49B, 3 UN Plaza, New York, NY 10017

United Nations Association–USA, 485 Fifth Avenue, New York, NY 10017

United Nations Information Center, 1889 F Street, N.W., Washington, DC 20006

United Nations Publications Sales Section, 2 United Nations Plaza, Room DC2-853, Dept. 421, New York, NY 10017

United States Arms Control and Disarmament Agency, 320 21st Street, N.W., Washington, DC 20451

United States Committee for UNICEF Education Program, 333 East 38th Street, New York, NY 10016

United States Department of State, Bureau of Public Affairs, Washington, DC 20520

United States Institute of Peace, 1550 M Street, N.W., Suite 700, Washington, DC 20005

World Bank, 4611-F Assembly Drive, Lanham, MD 20706–4391

Worldwatch Institute, 1776 Massachusetts Avenue, N.W., Washington, DC 20036

Cultural Diversity in the United States

5

The United States is a culturally diverse society. It is home to people of many different races, creeds, and ethnic origins. In the past, some have referred to the United States as a melting pot, which implies that each group loses its identity. On the contrary, it is more like a salad bowl or a patchwork quilt, because multiculturalism represents the idea that individuals keep their own ethnic group identity and at the same time function within the larger culture. Teaching multiculturalism also facilitates understanding of and respect for all individuals.

The United States is a nation of cultural pluralism. Indeed, many diverse individuals in the United States contribute to the microculture of our country. Because the United States is pluralistic, it is important that our schools become multiculturally aware, moving away from the traditional monocultural focus.

As educators, we must feel comfortable with our own cultural backgrounds and with the cultural backgrounds of our colleagues, parents, and students. We must use instructional strategies that help students value cultural diversity in our nation and at the same time realize that people across cultures have many similarities.

Culture determines the way we judge the world, and causes us to compare and judge other cultures through our own cultural perspective. When people are unable to view other cultures as equally worthy, they are ethnocentric. Ethnocentrism must be reduced and respect for other cultures must be increased. If students are to respect and value other cultures, they must become knowledgeable about them.

Engaging in theme immersions helps students become more knowledgeable about several cultures in the United States. The TIs in this section are the following: Native Americans, African Americans, Asian Americans, Latino Americans, and a general TI on cultural diversity.

Select Topic: Native Americans

All Americans are immigrants. Needless to say, Native Americans were the first; they came to this land from Asia thousands of years ago. They lived on the land long before Europeans and other immigrants came to the area we now know as the United States. They varied greatly in their own cultures, as they were shaped in large part by the varying physical environments.

When the Europeans arrived, new environmental factors were introduced that changed the land and the people. For example, new diseases introduced by the Europeans ravaged the Native Americans. The Europeans stripped the Native Americans of their land and their way of life.

The native peoples could not withstand the technology of the European invaders, such as the railroads for transportation, the telegraph for communication, modern weapons for destroying life, and the steel plow for cutting the prairies. Nevertheless, the legacy of the Native Americans remains in the names of our rivers, states, and cities. Their legacy remains in the lives of the Native Americans who are alive today. Their presence, past and present, enriches our nation, and they are a part of the rich tapestry of American life.

Make Lists and Web

If you and your students decide to study the topic of Native Americans, the next step is to assess your students' prior knowledge by asking them to tell what they know about Native Americans. We suggest a whole-class brainstorming session in which you make a list of what they know on a transparency or on the chalkboard. After this list is completed, encourage the class to ask questions about what they would like to know. The following may help you and your students as you make your own lists of "What we want to know."

What We Want to Know

- How long have Native Americans lived on the North American continent?

- What is the continental drift theory?

- What are some similarities and differences between the different groups of Native Americans in areas such as language, religion, housing, and work?

- Who are some major leaders of Native Americans?

- What are some major accomplishments of Native Americans?

- What was the policy of the United States government? How is it the same and different today?
- How did the genocide of the Native Americans occur? How was it justified by the European immigrants?
- What were major events in the history of Native Americans?
- What major battles were fought by Native Americans? Why?
- Why were Native Americans placed on reservations? What effect did this have on their lives?
- What treaties were made and were they broken? Why?
- How were Native Americans educated and what changes have been made in their education?
- What are some major contributions of Native Americans?

After the class has thought about what they want to know and the questions are formulated, it is time to organize the study. Ask the students to review all of their questions in order to develop a list of subtopics that represent the questions. Remind them that one question often relates to more than one subtopic. In the large group, guide students to generate a list. The following list of subtopics on Native Americans might give you ideas as you and the students generate your own list.

Subtopics on Native Americans

- Challenges of Native Americans, including poverty, education, discrimination, stereotypes, and health care
- Early history of Native Americans
- Number of tribes/bands in the continental United States
- Mexican Indians who migrated to the United States
- Similarities and differences of different groups of Native Americans
- Major leaders of Native Americans
- Major events involving Native Americans during the settlement of the United States
- Policy of the United States government toward Native Americans: past and present
- Famous Native Americans
- Reservations for Native Americans: purpose and results
- Genocide and Native Americans
- Wars involving Native Americans
- Major contributions of Native Americans

A list of subtopics has been decided and now a web can be made. Web the major subtopics that you and the students have identified and then add subordinate ideas to the subtopics. You will probably web on the chalkboard or overhead and then copy the final web on paper so that students can later refer to it.

Form Study Committees

After completing a web, the students should be organized into study committees. You and the students need to decide with whom students will work in their small groups and what topics they prefer to research. If you have a group of twenty-four students, for example, you might form six groups of four students in each group. In this case, you might limit the number of subtopics to six, with each group studying one of the subtopics.

Develop Questions

Students must be interested enough in a topic to raise questions and to explore those questions through research. Ask each group to develop as many questions as they can think of and then record them on a blank transparency so they can share them with the rest of the class and hear their comments.

If you have a study committee on the education of Native Americans (the first subtopic listed), the students might develop some of the following questions, or you might suggest that they research some of these questions.

Questions on Education of Native Americans

- Who decided how Native Americans would be taught, and why?
- How were the educational programs funded, and how much funding were they given?
- What is the view of Native Americans toward their education?
- Why has the Bureau of Indian Affairs insisted that Native Americans stay at boarding schools?
- What recent changes have been made in the education of Native Americans?

Study Topic

Once students have identified questions relevant to their topic, they begin the study. As students engage in study, they will add questions and delete some of the original ones. They use many resources, including books, nonprint sources, magazines and newspapers, and computers.

Fiction Trade Books

Ahyoka and the Talking Leaves by Peter Roop and Connie Roop. New York: Lothrop, Lee & Shepard, 1992. [I] This is a fictionalized account of Sequoyah and his daughter, the only Native American individuals known to have created a written language. It describes their hardships and their commitment to the task.

Eyes of Darkness by Jamake Highwater. New York: Lothrop, Lee & Shepard, 1985.[MS] A compelling and dramatic story of a young Native American caught between the world of his forefathers and the modern world. After receiving medical training in the white man's world, he returns to the reservation.

Nonfiction Trade Books

The Ancient Cliff Dwellers of Mesa Verde by Caroline Arnold, photographs by Richard Hewett. Boston: Clarion, 1992. [I] The reader is taken through Mesa Verde National Park to see the cliff dwellings and learn about the complex culture of the Anasazi Indians. Also presented are theories surrounding the disappearance of the Anasazi.

Anna's Athabaskan Summer by Arnold Griese, illustrated by Charles Ragins. Honesdale, PA: Boyds Mills Press, 1995. [I] Anna is a Native American who each summer goes with her family to the fishing camp to experience the culture of her ancestors, the Athabaskan Indians. Because of her summer experiences, she begins to understand the cycle of life.

Arctic Hunter by Diane Hoyt-Goldsmith, photographs by Lawrence Migdale. New York: Holiday House, 1992. [I] Reggie, an Inupiat Indian, spends the summer in a camp with his family hunting and fishing for food they will take back to the village. Includes lots of information about Inupiat life and their combination of traditional and modern lifestyles.

Arctic Memories by Normee Ekoomiak, illustrated by Normee Ekoomiak. New York: Henry Holt, 1991. [I/MS] Ekoomiak's artwork and the bilingual text bring to life a culture that is all but extinct. The author, an Inuk born near James Bay in Arctic, Quebec, tells stories and depicts scenes from his childhood.

Battlefields and Burial Grounds: The Indian Struggle to Protect Ancestral Graves in the United States by Roger C. Echo-Hawk and Walter R. Echo-Hawk. Minneapolis: Lerner, 1994. [MS] Describes Native Americans' attempts to reclaim artifacts from museums and other institutions and to rebury remains of their ancestors. Particular emphasis is given to the Pawnee.

Children's Atlas of Native America. Chicago: Rand McNally, 1992. [I/MS] Focuses on the first inhabitants of the Americas. Leads the reader on a geographic tour of the Americas and contains full-color maps and authentic photographs.

Clambake: A Wampanoag Tradition by Russell M. Peters, photographs by John Madama. Minneapolis: Lerner, 1992. [I] This book is part of the We Are Still Here series, which focuses on contemporary Native Americans. Stephen, a twelve-year-old Wampanoag, learns from his grandfather how to prepare and host the traditional ceremony of the Appanaug, or clambake.

Hiawatha: Messenger of Peace by Dennis Brindell Fradin. New York: McElderry, 1992. [MS] Learn about the real Hiawatha, who probably lived in the 1400s and whose life Fradin reinterprets. Hiawatha was a diplomatic leader and peacemaker who persuaded five warring tribes to create the Iroquois Federation.

An Indian Winter by Russell Freedman, illustrated by Karl Bodmer. New York: Holiday House, 1992. [I/MS] Freedman uses the journals of the German prince Alexander Philipp Maximilian and the sketches and paintings of Karl Bodmer to weave the story of the daily lives of the Hidatsa and Mandan peoples. The prince and the Swiss artist spent the winter of 1833–34 with the Hidatsas and Mandans in the Missouri River Valley in what is now North Dakota.

Let Me Be a Free Man: A Documentary History of Indian Resistance by Jane B. Katz (editor). Minneapolis: Lerner, 1975. [I] Traces the history of Indian resistance from 1607 through the Wounded Knee trial in 1974. This is an anthology of writings by Indians.

The Native American Almanac by Arlene Hirschfelder and Martha Kreipe de Montana. Cleveland: World Almanac, 1993. [I/MS] This excellent sourcebook covers all aspects of contemporary Native American life. It includes information about tribes, treaties, language, art, maps of tribal areas, and photographs.

Navajo-Visions and Voices Across the Mesa by Shonto Begay. New York: Scholastic, 1995. [I/MS] Begay's collection of twenty-one paintings gives glimpses of modern life on the Navajo reservation. Poems, stories, and Begay's personal memories are alongside each painting.

Pueblo Boy: Growing Up in Two Worlds, written and illustrated by Marcia Keegan. New York: Cobblehill, 1991. [I] Photographs and interesting, readable text reflect the life of Timmy Royal, a ten-year-old Pueblo Indian boy who lives in two cultures. He lives in New Mexico and his life is a mixture of mainstream American culture and Native American traditions.

Pueblo Storyteller by Diane Hoyt-Goldsmith, photographs by Lawrence Migdale. New York: Holiday House, 1991. [I] The life and customs of the Pueblo people are seen through the eyes of ten-year-old April, who lives with her grandparents. They live in the Cochiti Pueblo near Santa Fe, and her grandparents create the well-known clay storyteller figures.

Rising Voices: Writings of Young Native Americans, compiled by Arlene B. Hirschfelder and Beverly R. Singer. New York, Scribner, 1992. [MS] Through essays and poems, the young people in this excellent anthology tell about home, family, community, history, education, ritual, and their struggles for identity as they seek harmony in their two worlds. Each chapter has a short introduction and information about each author.

The Seminoles by Virginia Driving Hawk Sneve, illustrated by Ron Himler. New York: Holiday House, 1994. [I] This book takes the reader from the creation story to the present-day life of the Seminoles. The book is in the First Americans series.

This Song Remembers: Self Portraits by Jane B. Katz. Boston: Houghton Mifflin, 1980. [MS] Contains interviews with twenty Native American artists. Woodcutters, sculptors, poets, and others tell about the influence of their traditions upon their art.

Spirit Walker by Nancy Wood, illustrated by Frank Howell. New York: Doubleday, 1993. [MS] Nancy Wood's poems reflect the spirituality and teachings of the New Mexico Taos Indians. Howell's paintings are a perfect accompaniment.

Totem Pole by Diane Hoyt-Goldsmith, photographs by Lawrence Migdale. New York: Holiday House, 1990. [P/I] Aided by Migdale's photographs, young David, a member of the Tsimshian tribe, describes his father's step-by-step process of carving a totem pole. Explanations of the work as well as the traditions surrounding it are included.

The Village of Blue Stone by Stephen Trimble, illustrated by Jennifer Owings and Deborah Reade. New York: Macmillan, 1990. [I/MS] The daily life of the Anasazi pueblo dwellers is described and illustrated in pencil drawings. A year of seasonal rituals, social events, and daily tasks is recounted.

Express Knowledge

1. Make a list of states, cities, and rivers that have Native American names. It is interesting to note that more than half of the fifty states have Native American names. As you make your list, you might want to write a brief explanation that tells how and why the name was given.

2. Make maps of the United States that show the major groups of Native Americans at different times in the history of the North American continent.

3. Research different theories about how Native Americans migrated to America. Use maps to show the different theories.

4. Study ways Native Americans protected the environment. Compare their environmental practices with some of the bad practices of the past and with the good practices being advocated today.

5. Research one Native American reservation in the United States. Find out the following: employment opportunities on the reservation, problems facing the residents, natural resources, celebrations of the culture, and education of youth.

6. Investigate the population of Native Americans from the 1600s to the present. Make a list of the causes of death during the 1700s, 1800s, and 1900s. Make a graph to share your findings.

7. Imagine that you were forcibly displaced from the place where you lived, as many Native Americans were following the Indian Removal Act of 1830. Read accounts of the movement to reservations and Native Americans' feelings about the destruction of their highly developed societies.

8. Research the Bureau of Indian Affairs (BIA). Express your opinion as to whether the BIA has served the best interests of Native Americans.

9. Recommend ways in which local historical groups can preserve evidence of the culture of Native Americans. Send your recommendations to local groups.

10. Make lists of some of the several hundred Native American tribes/bands that lived in what is now the United States. Put an asterisk beside each tribe/band that was unfamiliar to you and research one.

11. Collect copies of texts and the names of movies and television shows that describe Native Americans as being the aggressors rather than defenders of their land. Make a poster that displays your findings.

12. Make recommendations about how to dispel misconceptions, such as the ideas that all Native Americans lived in tepees, used tom-toms, and wore headbands.

13. Collect from class members and resource persons in the school and community Native American artifacts such as baskets, pottery,

rugs, and ceremonial items. Display the artifacts in a classroom museum and invite other classes to view the collection.

14. Study the beadwork of some Native American tribes/bands. Find the supplies at a craft store and do a small replication of beadwork.

15. Find original Native American legends and study the origins of the people and animals. Read a legend to the class and share your knowledge of the characters.

16. Read about weaving designs of different Native American tribes/bands. Re-create some of the designs with paper or yarn.

17. Create Native American ledgers, which are pictures in bound books that record the person's thoughts and events in his/her life.

18. Research some aspect of Native American life, sequence the order of the events, and make colorful pictures. Make a cover and title page for the book that explains the illustrations.

19. Study the artistic objects that are important to the culture of tribes such as the Navajo, Haida, Hopi, and Zuni. Replicate some of the art forms from these tribes.

20. Critique the failure of the United States government to grant citizenship to Native Americans until 1924. Write a letter to the editor of a newspaper discussing this injustice.

21. Research American Indian calendars. Make a chart comparing their calendars with modern calendars.

22. Write a profile of a famous Native American, such as Dolley Smith Akers, Ben Black Elk, Black Hawk, Charles Carter, Cochise, Cornplanter, Crazy Horse, Geronimo, L. Rosa Minoka Hill, Napoleon B. Johnson, Chief Joseph, D'Arcy McNickle, Wilma Mankiller, Massasoit, N. Scott Momaday, Carlos Montezuma, Osceola, Pocahontas, Pontiac, Pope, Red Cloud, Sacagawea, Sequoya, Sitting Bull, Tecumseh, Little Turtle, or Pablita Velarde.

Select Topic: African Americans

African Americans were first brought to the colonies as captives. Although they came from many countries in Africa and from many cultures, most came from Central and West Africa. When the terrible trade in human cargo began in North America in 1619 and continued for over two hundred years, the raids on West Africa created chaos for the people living there. The stories of their capture, the long and deadly voyages to the New World, and their captivity stir strong emotional responses in us.

It is difficult to imagine how one group of people could consider another group of people to be inferior and enslave them for hundreds of years. With unending effort, African Americans struggled for freedom. They struggled and continue to struggle for their rights of life, liberty, and the pursuit of happiness, which are fundamental rights for all people.

As Walter Dean Myers writes in *Now Is Your Time: The African-American Struggle for Freedom* (HarperTrophy, 1991), "History has made me an African American. It is an Africa that I have come from, and an America that I have helped to create."

African Americans have contributed greatly to the quality of life in the United States. Martin Luther King, Jr., inspires us to value freedom for ourselves and for people throughout the world. His words in the "I Have a Dream" speech still ring in our ears and warm our hearts:

> When we allow freedom to ring, when we let it ring from every village and hamlet . . . we will be able to speed up that day when all of God's children . . . will be able to join hands and to sing in the words of the old Negro spiritual, "Free at last, free at last; thank God Almighty, we are free at last."

Make Lists and Web

What We Want to Know

- What was life like in West Africa before the slave trade to North America began?

- How and why did slavery occur in North America?

- What was the role of African Americans in the Revolutionary War?

- Why did the Constitution not abolish slavery?

- What famous American statesmen owned slaves?

- Why did slavery increase after the Revolution?

- What enabled African Americans to survive slavery?

- What was life like as a slave?

- Who were major African American abolitionists and what did they do?

- What role did African American churches have in the struggle for freedom and equality?

- What was the Emancipation Proclamation and what effect did it have?

- What were the contributions of African Americans during the Civil War?

- What happened to African Americans during Reconstruction?
- What was life like for African Americans in the South after Reconstruction?
- What were major accomplishments of African Americans after Reconstruction?
- When were there massive migrations of African Americans from the South and what were their destinations?
- What were major civil rights gains made by African Americans during the first half of the twentieth century?
- What were living conditions like in the cities of the North and Midwest?
- What effect did the Great Depression have on the lives of African Americans?
- What was the role of African Americans during World War II?
- How did civil rights activists work to achieve equality of African Americans during the 1950s and 1960s?
- Who were major leaders of the civil rights movement?
- What are some of the biggest challenges facing African Americans now and in the future?

Subtopics on African Americans
- Civil rights movement of the 1950s and 1960s
- West Africa before North American slave trade
- Development of slavery in America
- Role of African Americans in the Revolutionary War
- The Constitution and slavery
- Surviving slavery
- Major African American abolitionists
- Emancipation Proclamation
- Contributions of African Americans during the Civil War
- Reconstruction and African Americans
- African Americans in the South after Reconstruction
- Massive migrations of African Americans from the South
- African American life in northern and midwestern cities
- Role of African Americans during World War II and other wars such as the Korean, Vietnam, and Persian Gulf wars
- The Great Depression and African Americans
- Famous African Americans

- Challenges for African Americans now and in the future: family structure, poverty, racism, discrimination, and stereotypes

Form Study Committees and Develop Questions

Questions on Civil Rights Movement of the 1950s and 1960s

- What was the Brown v. Topeka Board of Education decision and what effect did it have on education?
- Why was the Montgomery bus boycott significant for the civil rights movement?
- How did Dr. Martin Luther King, Jr., emerge as the leader of the movement?
- What was King's philosophy of social change and how did he develop his views?
- What were some of the major events of the civil rights movement?
- What happened as a result of school desegregation?
- Who were some major civil rights leaders in addition to Dr. Martin Luther King, Jr., and what were their ideas and actions?
- What was the Voting Rights Act and what impact did it have on America?

Study Topic

Fiction Trade Books

The Captive by Joyce Hansen. New York: Scholastic, 1994. [I] This compelling novel follows a twelve-year-old Ashanti boy from his kidnapping in West Africa to his life as a slave in Salem, Massachusetts, and his subsequent freedom. It is told in the first person.

Cousins by Virginia Hamilton, illustrated by Jerry Pinkney. New York: Philomel, 1990. [I/MS] Cammy's two biggest problems are that her beloved Gran is in a nursing home and she just can't abide her too goody-goody cousin Patricia Ann. She sneaks into the nursing home to visit Gran, but only strong family love helps her resolve the tragic death of Patty.

The Dark Thirty: Southern Tales of the Supernatural by Patricia C. McKissack, illustrated by Brian Pinkney. New York: Knopf, 1992. [I/MS] This award-winning book consists of ten original stories that will definitely bring goosebumps—especially if you don't get home before "dark-thirty," thirty minutes before nightfall. The stories range from the days of slavery through the civil rights movement to the present time.

The Dream Keeper and Other Poems by Langston Hughes, illustrated by Brian Pinkney. New York: Knopf, 1994. [I/MS] This is a new and expanded edition of an inspirational book first published in 1932. Brian Pinkney's illustrations accompany each of Hughes's poems.

Freedom Songs by Yvette Moore. New York: Orchard Books, 1991. [MS] Set in the 1960s, this story follows fourteen-year-old Sheryl as she travels with her family from New York to North Carolina to visit relatives. She witnesses many social ills and returns to New York to work for civil rights.

Last Summer with Maizon by Jacqueline Woodson. New York: Delacorte Press, 1990. [I/MS] Margaret and Maizon are best friends in Brooklyn and the summer brings many changes to their lives. Margaret's father dies and Maizon receives a scholarship to an exclusive, predominantly White New England boarding school. How each girl copes and how their friendship survives forms the story in this well-written novel.

Letters from a Slave Girl: The Story of Harriet Jacobs by Mary E. Lyons. New York: Scribner, 1992. [MS] This is a fictionalized account of the life of Harriet Jacobs, a slave, and is based on the autobiography she published. Through fictional letters, Lyons tells the story of women in bondage and of Harriet running away after bearing two children to a White man.

Mississippi Bridge by Mildred Taylor. New York: Dial, 1990. [I] Jeremy, a ten-year-old White boy, is dismayed as he watches his Black neighbors being forced to leave a bus to make room for White passengers. Ironically, the bus crashes through the side of a bridge and Jeremy works with a Black man to help rescue passengers from the flood-swollen river.

Thank You, Dr. Martin Luther King, Jr.! by Eleanora E. Tate. New York: Watts, 1990. [I] Mary Elouise is in fourth grade and doesn't want to hear any more about being Black, and especially about things such as slavery and Dr. King. It's only after the storytellers come to her classroom and she listens to Imoni Afrika and then to her grandmother tell their proud stories that she begins her journey to self-discovery.

Toning the Sweep by Angela Johnson. New York: Orchard Books, 1993. [MS] The joy and pain of African American history is revealed in this coming-of-age story. Emily is fourteen and loves Grandmama and the desert, but her relationship with both is changing.

The Watsons Go to Birmingham by Christopher Paul Curtis. New York: Delacorte, 1995. [I/MS] Fourth-grader Kenny tells about his family, known as the Weird Watsons in Flint, Michigan, and about their summer vacation to Birmingham, Alabama, in 1963. This humorous adventure with some tense moments is about family love and endurance.

Nonfiction Trade Books

Against All Opposition: Black Explorers in America by Jim Haskins. New York: Walker, 1992. [MS] Did Africans explore the Americas before Columbus? Haskins presents evidence that they did and then provides short biographies of African Americans who explored various parts of the United States and beyond. Included are explorers as diverse as Jean Point du Sable, who founded Chicago, Estevánico, York, Matthew Henson, and present-day space explorers Guy Bluford, Jr., and Ronald McNair.

Black Dance in America: A History Through Its People by James Haskins. New York: Thomas Y. Crowell, 1990. [MS] Photos illustrate this history of Black dance in America, which begins with a description of "dancing the slaves" for exercise on slave ships. Dance companies, schools, choreographers, and dancers such as Bill "Bojangles" Robinson, Chubby Checker, and Katherine Dunham are introduced.

Black Stars in Orbit: NASA's African American Astronauts by Khephra Burns and William Miles. San Diego: Gulliver Books, 1995. [I] History of the United States space program from the perspective of African Americans. Provides a portrait of an amazing group of individuals.

Escape from Slavery: Five Journeys to Freedom by Doreen Rappaport. New York: HarperCollins, 1991. [I] True stories from the lives of fugitive slaves. Tells how both Black and White abolitionists helped courageous slaves escape to freedom.

The Forgotten Heroes: The Story of the Buffalo Soldiers by Clinton Cox. New York: Scholastic, 1993. [MS] Tells the little-known story of the Ninth and Tenth United States Cavalry Regiments, African American troops who were recruited by the government to protect western settlers. Illustrated with archival photographs.

The Great Migration: An American Story by Jacob Lawrence. New York: HarperCollins, 1993. [I] This significant book includes Lawrence's series of paintings of the northern migration of African Americans from the rural South. The book is augmented by a poem by Walter Dean Myers.

I'm Going to Sing by Ashley Bryan. New York: Atheneum, 1982. [I] Linoleum block prints illustrate this volume of Black American spirituals. Both words and music are included.

Jump at de Sun: The Story of Zora Neale Hurston by A. P. Porter. Minneapolis: Carolrhoda, 1992. [I] It's evident in this colorful biography how Zora Neale Hurston always remembered and practiced her mother's encouragement to "jump at de Sun!" This well-written biography brings the writer to life and introduces many of her stories, plays, and folktales.

Kids Explore America's African American Heritage by Westridge Young Writers Workshop. Santa Fe, NM: John Muir Publications, 1992. [I] This book tells about the history of African Americans from slavery through today. Aspects of the culture including art, music, dance, food, and celebrations are described. In addition, biographies of famous African Americans are included.

Kwanzaa: Everything You Always Wanted to Know but Didn't Know Where to Ask by Cedric McClester. New York: Gumbs & Thomas, 1990. [I] Relates how Kwanzaa is celebrated by African Americans between December 26 and January 1. The author explains the origins, principles, and practices of Kwanzaa.

Lessons from History: A Celebration in Blackness by Jawanza Kunjufu. Chicago: African-American Images, 1987. [I] Provides understanding about the rich history of the continent of Africa. In addition, great African Americans are highlighted.

Malcolm X: By Any Means Necessary by Walter Dean Myers. New York: Scholastic, 1993. [MS] Black-and-white photographs illustrate this well-written biography of Malcolm X. Myers details his life from childhood until his leadership of the Nation of Islam.

Master of Mahogany: Tom Day, Free Black Cabinetmaker by Mary E. Lyons. New York: Scribner, 1994. [I] The life and work of Tom Day, a free man in the era of slavery, are traced in this attractive volume. Day was a talented designer and furniture maker in North Carolina.

Now Is Your Time! The African American Struggle for Freedom by Walter Dean Myers. New York: HarperCollins, 1991. [MS] This well-documented book tells a rich history of African Americans from the time of the first slaves through the civil rights movement of the 1950s and 1960s. The book combines history, biography, and autobiography and includes many photographs and illustrations.

One More River to Cross: The Stories of Twelve Black Americans by Jim Haskins. New York: Scholastic, 1992. [I/MS] Twelve determined and talented African American men and women who made important contributions to American life are profiled in this book by Haskins. Learn about the lives of people such as Madame C. J. Walker, Charles Drew, Crispus Attucks, Marian Anderson, Jackie Robinson, Ralph Bunche, and others.

Our Song, Our Toil: The Story of American Slavery as Told by Slaves by Michele Stepto. Highland Park, NY: Millbrook, 1994. [I] These true stories are interesting and enlightening. Includes excerpts from narratives of the slaves and documentation of the contributions these men and women made to America.

Outward Dreams: Black Inventors and Their Inventions by Jim Haskins. New York: Walker, 1991. [I/MS] Brief biographical sketches acquaint the reader with little-known facts about African American inventors and their inventions. Many overcame prejudice to share achievements that made lasting contributions to life in America.

Rosa Parks: My Story by Rosa Parks with Jim Haskins. New York: Dial, 1992. [MS] It was on December 1, 1955, that Rosa Parks refused to give up her seat in the front of the bus to a White man in Montgomery, Alabama. Known today as the mother of the civil rights movement, Rosa McCauley Parks describes her upbringing in rural Alabama, her marriage, early involvement with the NAACP, and much more.

Sojourner Truth: Ain't I a Woman? by Patricia C. McKissack and Fredrick McKissack. New York: Scholastic, 1992. [I/MS] This excellent biography tells the story of Sojourner Truth, who was born into slavery but later became a famous abolitionist and advocate for women's rights. Brief biographical sketches of other pioneers in abolition and women's rights whom Truth knew are also included.

Stitching Stars: The Story Quilts of Harriet Powers by Mary E. Lyons. New York: Scribner, 1993. [I] This book in the African American Artists and Artisans series introduces Harriet Powers and her story quilts. Illustrated with full-color reproductions.

The Story of Negro League Baseball by William Brasher. New York: Ticknor, 1994. [I] This excellent book in the Baseball Legends series will appeal to young researchers interested in baseball and social history. The author brings to life men such as Leroy "Satchel" Paige and James "Cool Papa" Bell who played in the Negro Leagues.

Teammates by Peter Golenbock, illustrated by Paul Bacon. San Diego: Harcourt Brace, 1990. [I] This book describes the integration of professional baseball. The high point of the book is the day in 1947 when Brooklyn Dodger "Pee Wee" Reese stood up for his Black teammate, Jackie Robinson.

Thurgood Marshall: A Life for Justice by James Haskins. New York: Holt, 1992. [I] Thurgood Marshall was the first African American to sit on the United States Supreme Court. Using humor and anecdotes, Haskins tells Marshall's life story of concern for justice from his childhood to his years on the bench.

Express Knowledge

1. Research the African American business leaders in your community. Include the names of the businesses and information about them.

2. Write a report about the organizations that support African Americans in your community.

3. Create a bulletin board about leading African Americans in your state. Display pictures and information about them.

4. Make a chart that compares the West African empires of Ghana, Mali, and Songhai. Provide information on their leaders, major religions, lifestyles, families, work, and music.

5. Imagine that you are an African who was brought to America as a slave. Write an account of your voyage across the Atlantic.

6. Write a short, two-character play set in the United States during the days of slavery. You decide on the characters and the circumstances.

7. Research songs sung by African American slaves. Find recordings and/or sing some of the songs.

8. Write a newspaper editorial about an event that occurred during the days of slavery.

9. Develop a dramatic presentation of the Emancipation Proclamation to present to your class.

10. Write a letter to a friend describing Frederick Douglass or another famous African American abolitionist.

11. Write a song about the Underground Railroad. Sing it to your classmates.

12. Write a short autobiography as an African American immediately after the Civil War that describes how your life has changed after slavery.

13. Pretend that you are an African American child living in the South before the civil rights movement. Write several journal entries that reveal your thoughts and actions.

14. Conduct a pretend interview with a famous African American who showed courage during the civil rights movement. Ask classmates to contribute questions. Make a written or oral report about the results of the interview.

15. Read aloud a poem by a famous African American poet such as Maya Angelou, Eloise Greenfield, or Langston Hughes.

16. Write a travel article for an African American newspaper about Harlem during the time that Langston Hughes lived there.

17. Write a report that discusses the differences between the lives and work of African Americans in the 1970s and the early part of the twentieth century.

18. Write a profile of a famous African American such as Alvin Ailey, Muhammad Ali, Maya Angelou, Marian Anderson, Crispus Attucks,

James Baldwin, Mary McLeod Bethune, Gwendolyn Brooks, Ralph Bunche, George Washington Carver, Shirley Chisholm, Bill Cosby, W. E. B. Du Bois, Duke Ellington, W. C. Handy, Lena Horne, Langston Hughes, Jesse Jackson, Mahalia Jackson, Maynard Jackson, Mae Jemison, James Weldon Johnson, Barbara Jordan, Michael Jordan, Martin Luther King, Jr., Thurgood Marshall, Toni Morrison, Izaac Murphy, Jesse Owens, Rosa Parks, Sidney Poitier, Colin Powell, A. Philip Randolph, Paul Robeson, Jackie Robinson, Diana Ross, Wilma Rudolph, Robert Smalls, Mary Church Terrell, Jean Toomer, Harriet Tubman, Nat Turner, Booker T. Washington, Oprah Winfrey, Andrew Young, Whitney M. Young, or Malcolm X.

19. Make a chart that compares African Americans with the total U.S. population in several areas: population, annual family income, education, and occupations.

20. Make a map that shows the population distribution of African Americans today and make another map that shows the population distribution of African Americans many years ago.

21. Read folktales from Africa and identify the geographic origin, purpose, dilemma or conflict, characters, and moral or theme. Prepare a retelling to present to the class.

22. Find the 1963 Inauguration Day speech "Segregation Now—Segregation Forever" given by George Wallace. Write a rebuttal to the speech.

23. Read the speech "Letter from Birmingham City Jail" by Martin Luther King. Write your ideas about why this is one of the greatest letters in American history.

Select Topic: Asian Americans

A large number of Chinese workers came to America after the California Gold Rush in 1848 to work in mines and on the railroads. However, the Chinese Exclusion Act of 1882 prevented further entry of Chinese into the United States. Thereafter, landowners brought in Filipino, Japanese, and Indian workers. Later, in 1920, these and other Asians were also barred from entering the United States. There were, however, many Japanese and Korean women who entered the United States as wives of American servicemen after World War II.

In 1965, the immigration law changed, making it possible for large numbers of Asians to enter the United States. Thus, the Asian American population increased significantly from 1.5 million in 1970 to 7.3 million in 1990. Most Asian Americans are concentrated in several large cities such as Los Angeles and New York City.

Japanese Americans were the largest Asian American group in

1970. Today, however, Chinese Americans are the largest and Filipino Americans are the second largest. There have been few Japanese immigrants since 1965 because of the high standard of living in Japan. Since the standard of living is much lower in China, the Philippines, and other Asian countries, there has been a large influx of immigrants from those nations. In addition to the economic reasons for immigrating, there are other factors, such as politics. For example, since the fall of South Vietnam in 1975, about one million people from Vietnam and elsewhere in Indochina have entered the United States. Most of the Asian immigrants in the past two decades have urban backgrounds and are highly educated.

Although many Americans view all Asian Americans as a homogeneous group, there are many differences. Asian Americans have diverse languages, religions, national origins, and socioeconomic status.

Make Lists and Web

What We Want to Know

- What are some similarities and differences among Asian American groups?
- Why were most of the early Asian American immigrants men?
- What are some common stereotypes about Asian Americans? How and why did these stereotypes develop?
- What were the occupations of the early Asian Americans? How do these compare with those of contemporary Asian Americans?
- Why do Asian Americans immigrate to the United States?
- Where do most Asian Americans live? Why?
- How have Asian Americans been discriminated against?
- Has there been violence against Asian Americans? If so, what are some of those instances?
- Who are some famous Asian Americans?
- Why have many Asian American immigrants returned to their own countries? How does this compare with other immigrants, such as Europeans?
- What are some major immigration policies of the United States concerning Asian Americans?
- What are the lifestyles of Asian Americans?

Subtopics on Asian Americans

- Similarities and differences among Asian American groups
- Culture of individual groups including foods, language, religion, and family life

- Asian American stereotypes
- Occupations of Asian Americans: past and present
- Reasons for immigration
- Immigration policies: past and present
- Major population centers for Asian Americans
- Discrimination against Asian Americans
- Lifestyles of Asian Americans
- Famous Asian Americans

After the students have generated a list of subtopics, web ideas constructed by the students. You will probably web on the chalkboard and then copy the final web onto paper so that students can refer to it later.

Form Study Committees and Develop Questions

Questions on Discrimination Against Asian Americans

- What are some examples of anti–Asian American legislation?
- How did the U.S. government use one Asian group, such as the Filipinos, Japanese, or Chinese, to control another Asian group?
- Why were Asian Americans denied citizenship?
- What are some instances of violence toward Asian Americans? How did the Asian Americans respond?
- What were some early occupations of Asian Americans? How were the workers treated? How are those early occupations different from the occupations of Asian Americans today?
- What are some examples of segregation in housing and education for Asian Americans? What, if any, changes have been made regarding segregation and integration?
- Why were the Japanese Americans sent to internment camps during World War II? What happened to their property?

Study Topic

Fiction Trade Books

Ashok by Any Other Name by Sandra S. Yamate, illustrated by Janice Tohinaka. Chicago: Polychrome Publishers, 1992. [I] This book is about an eight-year-old boy of East Asian Indian descent who longs to change his name. His friendship with an African American teacher helps him understand that the first African Americans couldn't keep their names, and he learns to appreciate his name after all.

Blue Jay in the Desert by Marlene Shizekawa, illustrated by Isao Kikuchi. Chicago: Polychrome Publishers. 1993. [I] This story looks at the history of the Japanese American internment through the eyes of an eight-year-old child. The civil rights issues are addressed and the reader thinks about the Constitution and the Bill of Rights.

The Bracelet by Yoshiko Uchida, illustrated by Joanna Yardley. New York: Philomel, 1993. [I] Seven-year-old Emi and her family are Japanese Americans imprisoned in an internment camp. The author draws on her own childhood as a Japanese American to create an informative and inspirational story.

Hello, My Name Is Scrambled Eggs by Jamie Gilson. New York: Lothrop, Lee & Shepard, 1985. [MS] Tuan Nguyen and his family from Vietnam are sponsored by a church and will live with Harvey Trumble's family. Harvey looks forward to having "a kid of his own," but things aren't working out exactly like Harvey planned as Tuan Nguyen learns to be an American and still hold on to his Vietnamese culture.

Moon Lady by Amy Tan, illustrated by Gretchen Schields. New York: Macmillan, 1992. [I] One rainy afternoon, when Maggie, Lily, and June are bored, Grandmother tells them a story from her childhood in China. Wishes and a description of a traditional holiday are part of this story.

Nene and the Horrible Math Monster by Marie Villanueva, illustrated by Ria Unson. Chicago: Polychrome Publishers, 1993. [I] A story that addresses the myth that Asians can naturally do well in mathematics. Reading about Nene, a Filipino American girl in third grade, you realize that excellence in mathematics isn't genetic, but rather the result of much hard work.

The Star Fisher by Lawrence Yep. New York: Morrow, 1991. [MS] Teenager Joan Lee argues with her parents, who cling to Chinese traditions, and finds fitting in at school difficult. The story takes place in West Virginia in 1927 after the Lee family moved there from Ohio in search of a better life.

Stella: On the Edge of Popularity by Lauren Lee. Chicago: Polychrome Publishers, 1994. [I] This story is about a seventh-grade Korean girl named Stella Kim whose father owns a dry-cleaning establishment. Stella wants to be popular and yet balance family expectations, cultural values, and peer pressure.

Tales from Gold Mountain: Stories of the Chinese in the New World by Paul Yee, illustrated by Simon Ng. New York: Macmillan, 1990. [I/MS] Eight stories, based on rich folk traditions, tell of the difficult times faced by the first Chinese immigrants to North America. They worked on the railroads and in the gold mines overcoming great odds as they contributed to their new society.

Vatsana's Lucky New Year by Sara Gogol. Minneapolis: Lerner, 1992. [I] Her parents are Laotian, but Vatsana was born in America and sees no reason to learn Laotian customs. This is another book about the difficulties of learning to be part of two cultures.

Yang the Youngest and His Terrible Ear by Lensey Namioka, illustrated by Kees de Kiefte. Boston: Little, Brown, 1992. [I] The Yangs, a musically talented family, have recently moved from China to Seattle, where Mr. Yang is a music teacher. Mr. Yang cannot understand why Yingtoo, the youngest of the four children, just cannot make proper music on his violin, and it's very difficult to convince him that Yingtoo's talents lie in baseball.

Nonfiction Trade Books

Dan Thuy's New Life in America by Karen O'Connor. Minneapolis: Lerner, 1992. [I/MS] This photo essay is about thirteen-year-old Dan Thuy and her family. O'Connor uses black-and-white photographs and interviews to chronicle the life of a Vietnamese American family that has been in California only a short time.

El Chino by Allen Say. Boston: Houghton Mifflin, 1990. [I] Billy Wong, a Chinese American, aspires to be a great athlete. He becomes the first Chinese matador, but must first overcome obstacles placed in his path.

Famous Asian Americans by Janet Nomura Morey and Wendy Dunn. New York: Cobblehill Books, 1992. [MS] This interesting and informative book contains biographical sketches of fourteen distinguished Asian Americans. They represent a variety of Asian and Asian American cultural heritages and a wide range of professions.

Grandfather's Journey by Allen Say. Boston: Houghton Mifflin, 1993. [I] This beautifully illustrated book is a tribute to both Japan and America. Say ends the book with an expression that must be true for all who live or have lived in two worlds: "The moment I am in one country, I am homesick for the other."

I Am an American: A True Story of Japanese Internment by Jerry Stanley. New York: Crown, 1994. [I/MS] Stanley chronicles the plight of a Japanese American family during World War II. Included is a clear description of events leading up to the evacuation and internment of the Japanese Americans who lived on the West Coast.

The Invisible Thread by Yoshiko Uchida. New York: Julian Messner, 1991. [MS] In this autobiography, children's author Yoshiko Uchida tells what it was like growing up Japanese American in Berkeley, California, in the 1930s and 1940s. She and her sister viewed themselves as Americans, but others saw them as Japanese. Her family was among those sent to the Topaz internment camp in Utah when Order 9066 was issued after the bombing of Pearl Harbor.

The Journey: Japanese Americans, Racism and Renewal by Sheila Hamanaka. New York: Orchard, 1990. [I/MS] Hamanaka painted a twenty-five-foot, five-panel mural to reflect the experiences of Japanese Americans in twentieth-century America and especially of the Japanese, including members of her family, who were interned during World War II. This book was inspired by the mural and includes close-up photographs and a complete reproduction of the mural.

The Lost Garden by Lawrence Yep. New York: Julian Messner, 1991. [MS] This memoir by children's author Lawrence Yep recounts his years growing up as a Chinese American in San Francisco. He tells of being caught between two cultures and how these experiences influenced his writing.

A Pianist's Debut: Preparing for the Concert Stage by Barbara Beirne, photographs by Barbara Beirne. Minneapolis: Carolrhoda, 1990. [I] Leah Koon, an eleven-year-old Korean American pianist, tells about her daily life as she prepares to be a concert pianist. She and her grandmother move from California to New York in order for her to attend the Juilliard School of Music.

Express Knowledge

1. Make a bar graph showing the number of Asian American immigrants from 1850 through the present. You might want to make separate graphs for each major Asian American group.

2. Write a brief report about one or more of the following: California Miners' Tax, Chinese Fishing Tax, Chinese Exclusion Act of 1882, Alien Land Law, Geary Act of 1892, Gentlemen's Agreement of 1907–08, Immigration Act of 1917, Immigration Act of 1922, Executive Order 9066, Immigration Act of 1965.

3. Research the immigration of Asian Americans to the United States. What was the order of countries and provinces and how many immigrants came from each country?

4. Collect information on the immigration legislation that discriminated against Asians. List some of the laws, the year each law was passed, and the substance of the legislation.

5. Conduct a search to find out information on the occupational restrictions and problems faced by Asian Americans and their expulsion from some cities. Share your information in an oral report.

6. Describe the occupations of the first Asian Americans and the contributions they made to the prosperity of the United States.

7. Write a profile of a famous Asian American, such as José Aruego, Subrahmanyan Chandrasekhar, Michael Chang, Connie Chung, Fred Takahiro Hattori, Daniel K. Inouye, "Sox" Kitashima, Rose Hum Lee, Sammy Lee, Maya Ying Lin, Pardee Lowe, Yo Yo Ma, Oreme Matovodad, Irene Natividad, Dustin Nguyen, Ellison Onizuka, Seiji Ozawa, Ieoh Ming Pei, George Takei, Chang-Lin Tien, Yoshiko Uchida, Yung Wing, How Man Wong, Jade Snow Wong, Chien-shiung Wu, Taro Yashima, or Lawrence Yep.

8. Write a position statement about Executive Order 9066, which ordered the internment of many Japanese Americans in relocation centers during World War II.

9. Develop a speech on the suffering of the Japanese Americans between 1942 and 1945. Include facts about these citizens' economic losses and the psychological damage caused by being considered disloyal to the United States government.

10. Critique the fact that until 1924 Asian immigrants were ineligible for citizenship. Discuss how this lack of the ability to become a naturalized citizen was one of many obstacles facing immigrants from Asia.

11. Write a report on ways that Asian Americans helped to build the United States into a powerful nation.

12. Study the many different art forms from different countries and regions of Asia. Make a display of pieces of art or photographs of the art. Label each with the country or region of origin.

13. Discuss how life was probably more difficult for Asian immigrants than for European immigrants entering the United States. List some of the ways Asian Americans suffered "culture shock."

14. Research the Chinese zodiac, a twelve-year cycle that is dated after different animals. Find the year of the Chinese zodiac for each member of the class.

15. Study the artistic objects that are important to the cultures of Asia. Replicate some of the art forms.

Select Topic: Latino Americans

Latinos are the nation's second largest minority group; they comprise about 8 percent of the population. It is predicted that they will be the largest minority group after the turn of the century. Mexican Americans make up over half of the Latino population, followed by Puerto Ricans with about 15 percent, and Cubans with about 5 percent. Latinos of other backgrounds comprise the remaining population.

Needless to say, the history of Latinos in America differs significantly from one group to another. Cuban tobacco workers, for example, migrated to the United States in the late 1800s. The largest immigration of Cubans to the United States came after Fidel Castro's forces overthrew the Cuban government and established a Communist state. These later immigrants tended to be well educated and became affluent after living in the United States.

Puerto Ricans became citizens of the United States in 1917 with the passage of the Jones Act. There was only moderate immigration to the mainland until after World War II.

Mexican Americans in California and the Southwest were already living on the land when it became a part of the United States. Although the United States government guaranteed basic rights to the Mexican Americans, the policies and actions of the government caused small landowners to lose their land. In addition to the loss of land, Mexican Americans found themselves in an underclass status.

The Mexican American population continued to grow with the migration of people from Mexico. By 1920, a large number of Mexican immigrants had settled in many communities in the United States, working long hours for low pay. A high level of immigration occurred between the 1940s and 1980s. Later, legal immigration declined but undocumented migration continued at a high level. The immigration of Mexican Americans and other Latino groups parallels the massive immigration of Europeans that occurred, in large part, because of political and economic reasons.

Make Lists and Web

What We Want to Know

- What are some similarities and differences among Latino Americans?
- What happened to the Mexicans living in California and the Southwest after these areas became a part of the United States?
- Why did a large number of Mexicans, Puerto Ricans, and Cubans immigrate to the United States?
- What is life like for Latino Americans living in the United States?
- What are some forms of discrimination against Latino Americans? Why are they discriminated against? How does it compare with discrimination against other groups?
- What have Latino Americans done to overcome discrimination?
- Who are major Latino American leaders?

- What have been major immigration laws regarding Latinos?
- Why do some people refer to Latino Americans as Hispanics?
- What is the history of Latino Americans?

Subtopics on Latino Americans

- Culture, including family life, foods, language, and religion
- Similarities and differences among Latino Americans
- History of Mexican Americans, Puerto Ricans, and Cubans
- Reasons for immigration to the United States
- Immigration policies: past and present
- Occupations
- Discrimination and stereotypes
- Language policies: Spanish and English
- Famous Latino Americans

Develop Questions

Questions on Occupations

- How do occupations differ between the Latino American groups and the population at large?
- What changes have occurred with occupations of Latino Americans in recent years?
- Are workers organized into unions? Why? What are the results?
- In what ways have Latino Americans been discriminated against in their opportunities for work?
- How have Latino American workers contributed to the economic success of the United States?

Study Topic

Fiction Trade Books

Baseball in April, and Other Stories by Gary Soto. San Diego: Harcourt Brace, 1990. [I/MS] These eleven vignettes present details of daily life of children and teenagers in a Mexican American community in California. The stories are filled with warmth and humor.

Class President by Johanna Hurwitz. New York: Scholastic, 1991. [I] Readers may have met Julio Sanchez in other Hurwitz books, but in fifth grade Julio learns some different lessons. With the help of his new teacher, Ernesto Flores, Julio becomes proud of his name and of his Puerto Rican heritage.

Cool Salsa: Bilingual Poems on Growing Up Latino in the United States by Lori M. Carlson. New York: Holt, 1994. [MS] This bilingual collection of poems is a celebration of Latino American culture. A number of Hispanic writers share their experiences about growing up in America and tell how they attempt to merge their two cultures.

Family Pictures/Cuadros de Familia by Carmen Lomas Garza, illustrated by Carmen Lomas Garza. Emeryville, CA: Children's Book Press, 1990. [I] In this bilingual text, Lomas Garza recalls her childhood in Kingsville, Texas, near the Mexican border. Her bright and detailed drawings reveal much about her life, family, and the Hispanic American community.

Felita by Nicholasa Mohr. New York: Bantam Doubleday Dell, 1979. [I/MS] This story focuses on eight-year-old Felita and her relationship with her family and especially her beloved grandmother. Felita's family moves from a Puerto Rican barrio to a new neighborhood where they soon learn they're not wanted and must leave before someone is seriously hurt.

A *Fire in My Hands* by Gary Soto. New York: Scholastic, 1990. [MS] These twenty-three poems reflect the author's experiences growing up as a Mexican American in California's Central Valley. The themes are those that all children can relate to as they learn more about Hispanic culture.

Going Home by Nicholasa Mohr. New York: Dial, 1986. [MS] In this sequel to *Felita*, Felita is now twelve and goes to Puerto Rico to spend the summer with her uncle. She discovers her roots, but faces discrimination there for being a "nuyorican."

An Island Like You: Stories of the Barrio by Judith Ortiz Cofer. New York: Orchard Books, 1995. [MS] Stories about Puerto Rican immigrant youth caught between their families and the pull of the American dream. Readers get a real sense of a diverse neighborhood and its crowded streets.

Jesse by Gary Soto. San Diego: Harcourt, 1994. [MS] Set in southern California during the turbulence of the Vietnam War era, the story depicts the lives of Mexican Americans. Seventeen-year-old Jesse and his older brother attend community college hoping that education will improve their lives.

Journey of the Sparrow by Fran Leeper Buss with Daisy Cubias. New York: Lodestar, 1991. [MS] This well-written novel tells the poignant story of Maria and her two siblings, who flee El Salvador and illegally enter the

United States nailed in vegetable crates. They face many hardships as they try to make a better life for themselves in Chicago.

La Llorona: The Weeping Woman by Joe Hayes, illustrated by Vicki Trego Hill. El Paso, TX: Cinco Puntos Press, 1987. [I] The best-known folk story of Hispanic America. A scary story with mysterious events that imparts universal wisdom.

Latino Voices by Frances R. Aparicio. Highland Park: NJ: Millbrook, 1994. [MS] Biographical sketches of the Latino authors are included in this collection of fiction, nonfiction, and poetry. Important themes such as family, love, work, language, and race are addressed.

Lupita Mañana by Patricia Beatty. New York: Morrow, 1981. [MS] After the death of her father, thirteen-year-old Lupita travels to the United States with her brother. Although an undocumented worker and fearful of deportation, she must find work to help support her family left in Mexico.

Neighborhood Odes by Gary Soto, illustrated by David Diaz. San Diego: Harcourt, 1992. [I/MS] The twenty-one poems in this book focus on everyday events in the Mexican American neighborhood in central California where Soto grew up. Black-and-white drawings show contemporary Hispanic culture.

Pacific Crossing by Gary Soto. San Diego: Harcourt, 1992. [I/MS] When Lincoln Mendoza and his barrio brother Tony are selected as exchange students to Japan, they know little about what lies ahead of them. Lincoln, who is Mexican American, becomes a real member of his Japanese host family and learns to understand the similarities and differences between their lives.

Taking Sides by Gary Soto. San Diego: Harcourt, 1991. [I/MS] Lincoln Mendoza, an eighth-grade Mexican American, and his mother move from an urban barrio to a white suburb where life is very different. Lincoln has many worries, not the least of which is playing basketball against friends from his former school.

Nonfiction Trade Books

Day of the Dead: A Mexican-American Celebration by Diane Hoyt-Goldsmith, photographs by Lawrence Migdale. New York: Holiday House, 1994. [I] Day of the Dead is a holiday on which Mexicans with Indian backgrounds honor their dead. All the festivities of the holiday are told from the perspective of two Mexican American sisters.

Extraordinary Hispanic Americans by Susan Sinnot. Chicago: Children's Press, 1991. [MS] The author presents biographical sketches of Americans of Hispanic descent who have made important contributions to

North American culture. People from all walks of life and from the age of exploration into the twentieth century are included.

Famous Mexican Americans by Janet Morey and Wendy Dunn. New York: Cobblehill Books, 1989. [MS] Biographies of fourteen great Mexican Americans. The book addresses the prejudice they encountered as they attained success and acclaim for their accomplishments.

Fiesta: Cinco de Mayo by June Behrens. Chicago: Children's Press, 1978. [I] Mexico's day of independence from French occupation is celebrated on May 5 (Cinco de mayo), and September 16 (Dieciséis de septiembre) marks Mexico's independence from Spain. Readers will understand the reasons for celebrating both days and the differences between the two as they enjoy this photo essay capturing activities usually associated with the celebration of Cinco de mayo.

The Mexican American by Julie Catalano. New York: Chelsea House, 1988. [I] The lives of many great Mexican Americans are depicted. The book tells how Mexican Americans celebrate holidays and how they have gone from being the majority to the minority in the Southwest.

The Other Side: How Kids Live in a California Latino Neighborhood by Kathleen Krull, photographs by David Hautzig. New York: Lodestar, 1994. [I] A book in the World of My Own series. The story portrays the immigrant experience of three Latino American children.

Standing Tall: The Stories of Ten Hispanic Americans by Argentina Palacios. New York: Scholastic, 1995. [I/MS] David Farragut, the first admiral of the Navy, baseball hero Roberto Clemente, and singer Gloria Estefan are three of the influential Hispanic Americans whose stories are told in this book. Black-and-white photographs of each figure are included.

Express Knowledge

1. Write a report on one of the support groups for Latino Americans: American Civil Liberties Union; La Asociación Nacional México-Americana; Mexican-American Political Association; National Coalition for Fair Immigration Laws and Practices; National Farm Labor Union.

2. Research the powerful empires that existed in Central and South America. Create a timeline that illustrates many of the accomplishments of the civilizations.

3. Write a biography of the life of a Latino American, such as Everett Alvarez, Toney Anaya, Antonio Lópezde, Jerry Apodua, Romano A. Banuelos, Vikki Carr, Raul H. Castro, Cesar Chavez, Henry G. Cisneros, Roberto Clemente, Bert Corona, Justo S. Cruz, Ernesto Galarza, Hector P. Garcia, Eligio de la Garza, Ralph Guzman, Wilma

Martinez, Joseph Montoya, Katherine D. Ortega, Jesus Pallares, Tomás Rivera, Antonio Rodriguez, Linda Ronstadt, Edward R. Roybal, Phillip V. Sánchez, Lee Trevino, Luis Valdez, or Vincente T. Ximenes.

4. Conduct a study of Latino American culture, including language, religion, art, food, dances, and costumes.

5. Collect statistics about how many Latino Americans live in the United States, their country or territory of origin, the languages they speak, and their major religion. Graphically represent the information.

6. Read about the Mexican War. Analyze why the brutal massacres of Mexicans occurred and share the outcome of the war.

7. Investigate how the United States took Mexican territory that is now much of the Southwest. Find out how many states were Mexican territory in the early 1800s, the time they became states, reasons the United States wanted the territory, and the leaders in the movement.

8. Learn about the Texas invasion and the story of the Alamo. View the conflict from the perspectives of both Mexico and the United States.

9. Find examples of the legislation that has sought to control immigration of Latinos. Discuss the discrimination against Latinos in the legislation.

10. Explain some of the challenges that Latino Americans have endured in the United States. Include working conditions, housing, political representation, economic exploitation, poverty, education, unemployment, and English-only policies.

11. Stage a Latino American celebration. Study the costumes, dances, and foods that might be eaten at the celebration.

12. Conduct a study of Latino American music. Include the styles, the countries associated with the styles, musical composers, and famous musicians.

13. Collect information about Latino American dances. Include information on the types of dances, the dance patterns, and the countries associated with the dances.

14. Research Cinco de mayo, one of the major patriotic holidays celebrated in Mexico and in the United States by Mexican Americans. Plan a celebration in your classroom that has some of the usual aspects of the holiday.

15. Study the origins of Latino Americans. Construct a bar graph that

shows the percentage who are of Puerto Rican, Cuban, Mexican, Central American, and South American origin.

16. Find population statistics about the numbers of Latino Americans in different cities and states in the United States. The statistics may be reported according to the major groups: Cubans, Chicanos/Mexicans, and Puerto Ricans.

Select Topic: Other Americans

Americans have immigrated from almost every part of the world. Europeans are the largest group of immigrants to the United States. We provide the following TI that is general so that you and your students can apply it to any cultural group in the United States, including European Americans and a specific group of European Americans such as Swedish people.

Make Lists and Web

What We Want to Know

- Why did this group of people immigrate to the United States?
- What was the immigration policy regarding this particular group? Why?
- How did they travel to the United States? What were the travel conditions like?
- What happened to the immigrants when they arrived in the United States?
- What parts of the United States did they settle in?
- Were these people discriminated against in the United States? If so, how and why?
- What contributions did they make to the development of the United States?
- Did these people maintain their cultural identification with their home country?
- What are the attitudes of people in this group toward people who belong to a different cultural group?

Subtopics on Other Americans

- Culture of the group, including family life, foods, language, and religion
- Cultural identification with home country
- Reasons for immigration

- Immigration policy toward this group
- Travel to the United States
- Treatment of this group in the United States
- Contributions of this group
- Famous people from the group

Form Study Committees and Develop Questions

Questions on Cultural Identification with Home Country

- Are foods eaten in the United States similar to the foods in the home country? If so, which ones?
- Has the group kept the same religion? Why?
- Is there an interest in tracing roots of the family through visits or other means with people in the home country? Why?
- Have people in the group maintained the language of the home country? Why?
- Are special holidays or events celebrated in the United States that reflect the home country?
- What values or beliefs, if any, are similar to those in the home country?

Study Topic

Fiction Trade Books

The Always Prayer Shawl by Sheldon Oberman, illustrated by Ted Lewin. Honesdale, PA: Boyds Mills Press, 1994. [I] This picture book is about Adam, a Jewish boy from czarist Russia. Because of fighting and lack of food, Adam and his parents immigrate. Before he leaves Russia, his grandfather gives him his prayer shawl, which remains with Adam throughout his life.

Brooklyn Doesn't Rhyme by Joan W. Blos, illustrated by Paul Birling. New York: Scribner, 1994. [I] This delightful book captures the life of Rosie and her family, who came from Poland to Brooklyn at the turn of the century. Rosie is in sixth grade and writes in her journal about herself and her extended immigrant family.

Letters from Rifka by Karen Hesse. New York: Holt, 1992. [I/MS] Rifka, a twelve-year-old Jewish girl, flees Russia in 1919 and shares her hopes, dreams, and heartaches through letters to her cousin Tovah in Russia. Because she has ringworm, her entrance into the United States is impeded, but she is finally reunited with her family.

Mary McLean and the St. Patrick's Day Parade by Steven Kroll, illustrated by Michael Dooling. New York: Scholastic, 1991. [I] Mary McLean and her family left Ireland during the potato famine and arrived in New York in 1849. Will Mary find the perfect shamrock so she can ride in the St. Patrick's Day parade in Mr. Finnegan's cart? Includes notes about Irish immigration and origins of the St. Patrick's Day parade.

The Wildflower Girl by Marita Conlon-McKenna. New York: Holiday House, 1992. [I/MS] This well-written novel focuses on orphaned Peggy O'Driscoll as she makes her way from Ireland to Boston in 1850. The reader will almost feel seasick, experience problems of immigration, and give a sigh of relief as Peggy's life in America begins to take shape.

Nonfiction Trade Books

Amish Home by Raymond Bial. Boston: Houghton Mifflin, 1994. [I/MS] Bial provides a sensitive and informative look into the lives of the Amish. There are no pictures of the Amish people, but color photographs by the author capture their spirit.

An Ancient Heritage: The Arab-American Minority by Brent Ashabranner, photographs by Paul S. Conklin. New York: HarperCollins, 1991. [I] This is an in-depth examination of one of our little-known ethnic groups. After a brief history of Arab Americans, the book includes personal stories of Arab American men and women from different parts of the country and different social strata.

Dancing to America by Ann Morris, photographs by Paul Kolnik. New York: Dutton, 1994. [I] In search of a better life, sixteen-year-old Anton Pankevich and his family left the former Soviet Union and traveled to New York. Anton is determined to become a top-flight dancer and studies at the School of American Ballet. He faces the same concerns that immigrants have always faced as he adjusts to a new country.

One World, Many Religions: The Ways We Worship by Mary Pope Osborne. New York: Alfred A. Knopf, 1996. [I/MS] The origins, traditions, sacred writings, forms of worship, and major holidays of Judaism, Christianity, Islam, Hinduism, Buddhism, Confucianism, and Taoism are explained. Many photographs, maps, and graphics enhance understanding of religions in the United States and the world.

Shaker Villages by Nancy O'Keefe Bolick and Sallie G. Randolph, illustrated by Laura LoTurco. New York: Walker, 1993. [I] This book provides an account of the history of this unique sect. Village architecture, production techniques, and a description of their daily routines are included.

Tracing Our Jewish Roots by Sagon Miriam. New York: Norton, 1993. [I/MS] Biographies of many European Jews who came to America. Jewish life in America from the early 1800s until today is discussed.

Express Knowledge

1. Dramatize the voyage of the immigrants to the United States.

2. Find songs that the immigrants sang or compose songs they might have sung on their voyage to their new country.

3. Conduct a nationality/ethnic origins survey of students and teachers in your school. Share the information through a school newspaper column or a bulletin board.

4. Create an idea about how local communities can actively foster the ethnic heritage of residents.

5. Survey class members, teachers, and others in your school to find the place in the United States where their ancestors first lived.

6. Communicate through the Internet with students your age who represent different cultural and ethnic groups. Summarize what you have learned from them.

7. Develop a web page for the World Wide Web that tells about the cultural or ethnic contribution to the United States, your state, and your community of one group of immigrants.

8. Summarize the contributions of one ethnic group to the building of the United States.

9. Write a profile of a famous American from the group you represent or are studying.

10. Research the leading members of the group you are studying. Include musicians, artists, athletes, scientists, writers, political leaders, and scholars. Find pictures and articles and create a bulletin board or poster on your findings.

11. Discuss ways in which immigrants from a country can keep their own culture, hold values that are unique to their ancestry, and yet live as Americans. Make a list of the ideas that resulted from your discussion.

12. Discuss ways that people can counter conscious and unconscious prejudice, stereotypes, and misinformation. Make a list of the recommendations that come from the discussion.

Resources
Professional Books for Teachers

The following books have been selected to support you as you deepen your knowledge about cultural diversity in the United States and to assist you in developing curriculum. Some books may contain information you can share with students by reading aloud or by sharing sections.

BAIRD, R. M., AND S. E. ROSENBAUM. 1992. *Bigotry, Prejudice, and Hatred: Definitions, Causes, and Solutions.* Buffalo, NY: Prometheus Books.

BARNES, D., ed. 1992. *Common Bonds: Anti-Bias Teaching in a Diverse Society.* Washington, DC: Association for Childhood Education.

BENÉT, S. V., AND R. BENET. 1984. *A Book of Americans.* New York: Henry Holt.

BIERHORST, J., ed. 1971. *In the Trail of the Wind: American Indian Poems and Ritual Orations.* New York: Farrar, Straus and Giroux.

CADUTO, M., AND J. BRUCHAC. 1988. *Keepers of the Earth: Native American Stories and Environmental Activities for Children.* Golden, CO: Fulcrum.

DERMAN-SPARKS, L. 1989. *Anti-Bias Curriculum.* Washington, DC: National Association for the Education of Young Children.

DUVALL, L. 1994. *Respecting Our Differences: A Guide to Getting Along in a Changing World.* Minneapolis: Free Spirit Publishing.

HARRIS, J. J., ed. 1992. *Teaching Multicultural Literature in Grades K–8.* Norwood, MA: Christopher-Gordon.

KLEINFELD, J. S., AND Y. S. KLEINFELD, eds. 1995. *Gender Tales: Tensions in the Schools.* New York: St. Martin's Press.

LINDGREN, M. V., ed. 1991. *The Multicolored Mirror: Cultural Substance in Literature for Children and Young Adults.* Fort Atkinson, WI: Highsmith Press.

LOPEZ, T. A. 1993. *Growing Up Chicano: An Anthology.* New York: Morrow.

MANNA, A. L., AND C. BRODIE, eds. 1992. *Many Faces, Many Voices: Multicultural Literacy Experiences for Youth.* Fort Atkinson, WI: Highsmith Press.

NIETO, S. 1992. *Affirming Diversity: The Sociopolitical Context of Multicultural Education.* New York: Longman.

READER'S DIGEST ASSOCIATION. 1978. *America's Fascinating Indian Heritage.* New York: Reader's Digest Association.

SLAPIN, B., AND D. SEALE, eds. 1992. *Through Indian Eyes: The Native Experience in Books for Children.* Berkeley, CA: New Society/Oyate.

SMITHSONIAN. 1978. *Handbook of North American Indians.* Washington, DC: Smithsonian.

STRYKER-RODDA, H. 1977. *How to Climb Your Family Tree for Beginners.* Arlington, VA: National Genealogical Society. (Resources on how to conduct genealogy research with many types of records.)

SZUCS, L. D. 1986. *Ellis Island, Gateway to America.* Arlington, VA: National Genealogical Society. (Describes tracing family history and how to determine if ancestors came through Ellis Island.)

VIGIL, A. 1994. *The Corn Woman: Stories and Legends of the Hispanic Southwest.* Englewood, CO: Libraries Unlimited.

Documents

Many primary source materials are available so students can see a copy of the original document, read the actual text, or see photographs and prints of an event. The following list represents some places to find primary sources. Many of the addresses are in the list at the end of this chapter or the list in Appendix A.

- American Museum of National History, Southwest Museum, and the Heye Foundation
  Reproductions of Native American photographs and slides
- Bureau of Indian Affairs, United States Government Printing Office Reservation maps and photographs of Native Americans
- Department of Anthropology, University of Chicago, Center for Study of Man
  Native American document reproductions
- Heard Museum, Phoenix, Arizona
  Large collection of print resources about Native Americans in the Southwest
- State historical societies
  Census records from the late 1800s that list the names of immigrants and the country of birth, and books written about the state that discuss the immigrants to the area

Selected Print

There are so many different series and individual books available that it is impossible to list all of them. We have included several that we would use in TIs.

- Children's Press
  A New True Book series that includes *The Navajo* and *The Anasazi* (photographs appropriate for intermediate students)
- Cobblestone Publishing Company
  Three journals that have current issues and back issues about cultural diversity in the United States: *Cobblestone*, *Faces*, and *Calliope*
- Cookbooks
  Available on most ethnic and cultural groups
- Greenhaven Press
  Series that promote social interaction: Opposing Viewpoints Junior series: *Immigration*; Overview series: *Illegal Immigrant* and *Immigration*; World History series: *Traditional Africa* and *Traditional Japan*
- Heard Museum
  Many books, including two books by Susan L. Shaffer and others, *O'odham: Indians of the Sonoran Desert* and *Hopi: The Desert Farmers* (1989)

- Knowledge Unlimited
  Posters that celebrate diversity in the United States

- Lerner Publications
  Several series that include We Are Still Here: Native Americans Today; and In America Books. Magazines about African Americans include *Jet*, *Ebony*, *Essence*, and *Black Child*

- Modern Curriculum Press
  Books and posters in a series titled Voices in African American History

- National Women's History Project
  Photo display set that includes American women

- Steck-Vaughn Publishers
  Multicultural America series, which includes *The Westward Movement and Abolitionism* and *Great Migrations, 1880–1912*

- Teaching with Historic Places
  Plans for teaching about the following places in African American history: *Chicago's Black Metropolis*; *Glen Echo Park*; *Montpelier: James and Dolley Madison*; *Old Court House* in St. Louis; and *Vieux Carre: Creole Neighborhood*; plans for teaching about the following places in Hispanic-American history: *California to America: Cultural Change*; *Castolon: Meeting Two Cultures*; *San Antonio Missions*; and *Ybor City: Cigar Capital*

Media

Many wonderful videotapes, audio recordings, maps, posters, and much more are available from a variety of resources. We have listed a few that we have examined, but many more exist.

- Children's Book and Music Center
  Books and audiocassettes on African-American culture, including folktales and songs

- Frontier Software
  Software on African Americans

- Knowledge Unlimited and Filmic Archives
  Videocassettes on different ethnic and cultural groups in the United States

- Library Video Company
  Ten videocassettes in the "Hispanic & Latin American Heritage Collection" on Joan Baez, Simón Bolívar, Cesar Chavez, Roberto Clemente, Hernando Cortes, Ferdinand and Isabella, Pablo Neruda, Juan and Evita Perón, George Santayana, and Pancho

Villa; and a series titled *Multicultural Peoples of North America: Mexican Americans, Puerto Ricans, and Central Americans*

- Native Voices Public Television
  Series on Native Americans that includes *Without Reservations, Ernie Pepion and the Art of Healing, What Shamans & Plastic Medicine Men, The Crow-Mapuche Connection, Warrior Chiefs in a New Age, Transitions,* and *The Place of the Falling Waters*

- Recorded Books
  Books on tape include *Anpao* (Jamake Highwater), *Frederick Douglass* (William S. McFeely), *Let the Circle Be Unbroken* (Mildred D. Taylor), *Maya Angelou* (Miles Shapiro), *To Be a Slave* (Julius Lester)

- Schlessinger Video
  Video titled *Holidays for Children: Cinco de Mayo*

- SRA School Group
  Videocassette of *Diego*

- SSSS (Social Studies School Service)
  Catalog lists many different media available on several ethnic and cultural groups from within the United States

- World Almanac Education
  Video titled *A History of Native Americans*

Technology

Since use of the computer expands each day, it is impossible to list current individual programs and World Wide Web sites about cultural diversity in the United States.

- World Wide Web sites
  Ethnic and cultural celebrations, personalities, history, and interviews

- Internet/e-mail
  Correspond via e-mail with individuals of all cultures and ethnic groups in the United States

- Knowledge Unlimited
  CD-ROM on different ethnic and cultural groups within the United States

People

Every community has individuals who are knowledgeable on ethnic diversity in the United States. As you know, they can be found near the school (parents, staff members, and community members), in private and public agencies, and at local universities and colleges. We have listed some of the people we would invite to speak to our students.

- All ethnic groups
- Foreign-born members of the community
- Locally recognized authorities
- Craftspersons
- Local artists
- Art teacher knowledgeable about art of particular cultures
- Native American
- Indian Council chairpersons or spokespersons
- Member of the Bureau of Indian Affairs Land Management Office

Interview Question Ideas

The following interview questions are meant to be a beginning point as your students develop questions of their own.

Interview with a Native American

- Can you tell me anything about the early history of your tribe/band?
- What is the language of your tribe/band?
- Can you tell me any of the legends of your tribe/band?
- What is the political structure of your tribe/band?
- How do your tribal laws differ from those of the U.S. government?
- What is the role of women in your tribe/band?
- What are the customs concerning the treatment of elderly people in your tribe/band?
- Are there any special foods that originated from your tribe/band?
- What are the celebrations of your tribe/band?
- Do you have any family heirlooms that were made by your ancestors?
- How do you feel about the way Native Americans have been treated by the U.S. government?
- Where did your tribe/band live before European settlers came to this country?
- Can you tell me any of the history associated with the treatment of your tribe/band?
- Was your tribe/band ever placed on a reservation?

Interview With a Member of an Ethnic Group

- How many generations has your family lived in this country?
- Do you know anything about the family members who came to this country first?
- How many members of the family came?
- Do you know about their occupations?
- Where did they first live in the United States?
- Have they moved around the United States?
- Do they carry on any of the customs from the "old" country?
- Do you know about relatives who still live in the "old" country? If yes, have any of the family members visited them or have they visited the United States?
- In what ways do your family members reflect their ethnic heritage?
- Do you eat food that reflects your heritage on a regular basis or on holidays?
- Do you celebrate any of the holidays associated with your heritage?
- Are there any artifacts in your home that reflect your heritage?
- Are there any special costumes that are used for special occasions?
- Is there anything unique about your birth, marriage, or death rituals?
- What about your life most reflects your cultural heritage?

Interview Questions for Someone Who Has Immigrated to the United States but Has Lived in the United States for Many Years

- Tell me about your country.
- Were you born there?
- How many years did you live in that country?
- How does that country differ from where you live now?
- Tell me about customs that are different from those in the United States.
- What do you miss?
- Is there anything that you like better in the United States?
- What holidays do you celebrate that aren't celebrated in the United States?
- How did people earn a living?
- Has that country been in any wars during your life?
- Did anything happen to your family during the war?

- Describe your daily life.
- Describe the government.
- Who were some of the government leaders that you remember?
- Did you become a U.S. citizen?

Interview Questions for Someone Who Recently Immigrated to the United States

- What country did you live in before coming to the United States?
- Why did you leave?
- What were some of the problems in your country?
- Is there ample food in your country? If no, why are there shortages?
- Is there a clean water supply in your country? If no, why isn't the water pure?
- What is the condition of the roads in your country?
- What are some of the things that you miss from your country?
- Did you leave family members or close friends behind? If yes, tell me about them.
- How did you feel when you left your homeland?
- Did you have any hopes or dreams for your new life in the United States?
- What kind of transportation did you use to get to the United States?
- Was it difficult to get a visa?
- Was it difficult funding the transportation to the United States?
- Did you have any difficulty with immigration?
- What was your port of embarkation from your home country and what city did you come into in the United States?
- What had you heard about the United States?
- Did you know anyone in the United States? If yes, whom did you know?
- In what ways was the education in the United States similar to or different from that in your home country?

Family History

Family and oral history research are very similar in the way they are conducted. We have listed them separately but we encourage you to refer to the information in both sections. See Appendix E for information on conducting family history research.

Many families can trace their ancestors back to another country. Recording memories and information about one's family is a great gift to future generations.

Except for Native American families, most families have immigrated from another country at some time since the early 1600s. Suggest that students investigate the family ethnic heritage in the following ways:

- Interview family members about the ethnic heritage of the family. Develop a family tree that not only gives the names of ancestors but also gives their place of birth. Many Americans can trace their family tree back to several countries.
- Ask older family members to help you determine if any of the family customs can be traced to origins in another country.
- Ask family members about artifacts that have been in the possession of the family that reflect their ethnic or cultural heritage.
- Take photographs of the items and make a scrapbook. Ask an older family member to help write captions for the photographs.
- Develop a genealogical chart.

Before beginning a family interview, ask the person to give his/her name, birth date, and place of birth, and to name parents and brothers and sisters.

Suggested Questions

- Where did the family live?
- Will you describe the home? (apartment, house, etc.)
- Who lived in the home?
- Did grandparents live in the home? If no, where did grandparents and other older family members live?
- How did the family feel about elderly family members?
- Did married children live in the home?
- At what age did young people marry?
- Was the home crowded?
- Did any other family members live near them?
- Did the family own the home?
- What work did your mother and father do?
- What work did women do outside the home?
- How did the family feel about women's work?
- Did children go into the same work as the mother and father?
- How many days each week did family members work?

- How were the clothes washed?
- What kind of food did the family eat?
- Who cooked the food?
- Who did the household work?
- Where did the people sleep in the home?
- What did the family do for recreation?
- What toys did the children have?
- What did teenagers do for fun?
- How long did most family members go to school?
- What were the family celebrations?
- Did the family observe religious holidays?
- What were the family wedding customs?
- What were the family funeral customs?
- If the family moved, what was the reason?
- How far back on both sides of the family can ancestors be traced?

Oral History

Oral history ideas are included that can be photocopied and given to students to serve as a springboard for the development of their questions. Because oral and family history research have similarities, we encourage you to read the family history section of this chapter. Refer to Appendix E for information on conducting oral history research.

Many communities haven't compiled the contributions of ethnic groups to their history. During the depression years of the 1930s, there were public works projects that made records of those who settled in different areas of the United States. Find gaps that exist in the history of your community.

Many of the same questions that are listed under family history can be adapted for use in an oral history project concerning the contributions of different ethnic groups. Additional questions might include the following:

- When did your family settle in this community?
- Why did they move here?
- Were they the first members of the _____ community?
- Were they welcomed by the other members of the community?
- What are some of the things that the members of the _____ community did? (Build streets or buildings, teach school, start a church, etc.)

- Where were members of the _____ community buried?
- Do you know how large membership in the _____ community is today?
- Did members of the _____ community retain any of the traditions of their previous home?
- Do any celebrations take place within the _____ community?

Field Trips

In many communities, there are places where students can increase their understanding of different ethnic and cultural groups. A few suggestions follow for learning about members of groups that immigrated from other countries.

- Street fairs and ethnic festivals
- Historical societies to study early population records and countries of origin
- Museums and galleries for displays of art done by members of the group
- Recitals, dance performances, and musical concerts by performing groups from the culture
- Religious celebrations
- Storytelling festivals by members of the culture
- Ethnic food stores

Suggestions for Places to Visit to Increase Understanding and Appreciation of Native American Culture

- Old missions
- Archaeological excavations
- Museums with Native American displays
- Native American centers
- Powwows and other Native American celebrations
- Historical societies to see documents, historical writings, and treaties

Fantasy Field Trip Suggestion

1. Choose an ethnic celebration that you would like to attend.
2. Research the details of the celebration and find out if there is music or dancing.
3. Find pictures of the city or place, the costumes that are worn, and the activities of the people. See if a videotape is available.

4. Investigate transportation to the city or area and the local transportation and pretend to make reservations.

5. Learn about places to stay in the community and pretend to make reservations.

6. Investigate the food that will be served. Find recipes and plan to cook the food at school or home on the day of the event.

7. Schedule the day of the celebration and decorate the classroom.

8. Hold the celebration, pretend to go there, pretend you are dressed in costumes as you look at photographs, listen to music, eat the food, and return home.

Art

When studying the art of any culture or country, develop an understanding and appreciation of the aesthetic contributions. For instance, a study of Asian American art would not be complete without giving attention to architecture, carved jade, chinoiserie, and gardens.

It is especially important when studying Native Americans that students be aware that different tribes/bands each had different objects of art, including their baskets, pottery, clothing, rugs, and ceremonial items. When replicating any articles used for worship, remind students that the objects are for a serious purpose and shouldn't be ridiculed in the classroom.

- *American Artists Reflect American History Series*, Vol. I: Native Americans. Cypress, CA: Creative Teaching Press (set of reproductions of famous artworks by Native American artists)

- Art Education Inc.
  Full-color reproductions of Chumash basket and cover, Mandan painted shield, and Navajo blanket

- Art Image Publications, Inc.
  Full-color reproductions of many different Native American family scenes, ceremonies, and chiefs

- Knowledge Unlimited
  Set of posters that celebrate ethnic diversity, including "Cultural Rainbows: An American Alphabet," "African American Artists," "Contemporary Native Americans," "Great Asian Americans," "Hispanic Americans," "Hispanic Heritage," "Native American Cultures," "Struggle for Civil Rights," and "Voices of Diversity"

- Manley, Ray. 1979. *Ray Manley's Collecting Southwestern Indian Arts and Crafts*. Tucson: Ray Manley Photography (photographs of baskets, jewelry, rugs, and kachina dolls)

Music

Almost every ethnic and cultural group in the United States has some music that is unique to it. Public libraries often have collections of recordings representing many groups. Resource people from the group can tell you where you can locate music and musical instruments.

- McLaughlin, Roberta. 1990. *American Indian Songs*. Van Nuys, CA: Alfred Music Publishers
- Penton Overseas
  Lyric Language Live Action Music Video: A Bilingual Music Program, in Spanish or English

Addresses

The addresses in this section are provided because each is a source for information or materials related to cultural diversity in the United States. Because addresses change, consult the *Encyclopedia of Associations* found at many public libraries for current addresses.

American-Arab Anti-Discrimination Committee, 4201 Connecticut Avenue, N.W., Suite 500, Washington, DC 20008

American Civil Liberties Union, 132 West 43rd Street, New York, NY 10036

American Friends of the Anne Frank Center, 106 East 19th Street, Fourth Floor, New York, NY 10003

American Jewish Committee, Institute of Human Relations, 165 East 56th Street, New York, NY 10022

Anti-Defamation League of B'nai B'rith, 823 United Nations Plaza, New York, NY 10021

Army Map Service, San Antonio Field Office, Building 2011, Fort Sam Houston, TX 78234

Asia Society, 925 Park Avenue, New York, NY 10021

Bureau of Indian Affairs, Department of the Interior, Washington, DC 20240

Center for Democratic Renewal, P.O. Box 50469, Atlanta, GA 30302

Commission on Civil Rights, 1121 Vermont Avenue, N.W., Washington, DC 20425

Congressional Black Caucus, 344 House Office Building, Annex 2, Washington, DC 20515

Congressional Hispanic Caucus, 557 House Office Building, Annex 2, Washington, DC 20515

Council on Islamic Education, P.O. Box 20186, 9300 Gardenia Street, Fountain Valley, CA 02728-0186

Equal Employment Opportunity Commission, 1801 L Street, N.W., Washington, DC 20507

Greenfield Review Press, 2 Middle Grove Road, P.O. Box 308, Greenfield Center, NY 23833

Immigration and Naturalization Service, 425 I Street, N.W., Washington, DC 20536

National Archives, General Services Administration, Washington, DC 20540

National Association for the Advancement of Colored People, 186 Remsen Street, Brooklyn, NY 11201

National Women's History Project, 7738 Bell Road, Windsor, CA 95492

Native Voices Public Television, 222 Visual Communications Building, Montana State University, Bozeman, MT 59717

Superintendent of Documents, Government Printing Office, Washington, DC 20402

Addresses

American Library Color Slide
   Company
P.O. Box 5810
Grand Central Station, NY 10163-5810

American Peace Society
4000 Albemarle Street, N.W.
Washington, DC 20016

Asia Society
725 Park Avenue
New York, NY 10021

Asian-Pacific Heritage Council
Box 11036
Alexandria, VA 22312

Association on American Indian
   Affairs
245 Fifth Avenue
New York, NY 10016

Association for the Study of Afro-
   American Life and History
1401 14th Street, N.W.
Washington, DC 20005

Bureau of Engraving and Printing
14th and C Streets, S.W.
Washington, DC 20228

California Department of Education
P.O. Box 944272
Sacramento, CA 94244-2720

Center for Folklife Programs and
   Cultural Studies
955 L'Enfant Plaza, S.W., Room 2600
MRC 913, Smithsonian Institution
Washington, DC 20560

Center for Teaching About China
1214 West Schwartz
Carbondale, IL 62901

Center for United States–Mexican
   Studies
D-010 University of California–San
   Diego
La Jolla, CA 92093

Children's Book and Music Center
2500 Santa Monica Boulevard
Santa Monica, CA 90404

Cobblestone Publishing Company
7 School Street
Peterborough, NH 03458-1454

Committee on Teaching About Asia
5633 North Kenmore #24
Chicago, IL 60660

Council on Interracial Books for
    Children
1841 Broadway
New York, NY 10023

Creative Teaching Press
P.O. Box 6017
Cypress, CA 90630-0017

Filmic Archives
Cinema Center
Botsfort, CT 06404-0386

Frontier Software
P.O. Box 56505
Houston, TX 77227

Global Education Associates
475 Riverside Drive, Suite 456
New York, NY 10115

Global Perspectives in Education
218 East 18th Street
New York, NY 10003

Government Printing Office
Superintendent of Documents
Washington, DC 20402

Greenhaven Press, Inc.
P.O. Box 289009
San Diego, CA 92198-0009

Hartley Courseware Inc.
133 Bridge Street
Dimondale, MI 48821

Heard Museum
11 East Monte Vista Road
Phoenix, AZ 85004

IBM Corporation
P.O. Box 1328-W
Boca Raton, FL 33429-1328

Jackdaw Publications
P.O. Box A03
Amawalk, NY 10501

Knowledge Unlimited
P.O. Box 52
Madison, WI 53701-0052

Korean War Veterans Memorial
18th and C Streets, N.W., Room 7424
Washington, DC 20240-9997

Library of Congress,
National Archives, NEPS-Dept. P491
P.O. Box 100793
Atlanta, GA 30384

Library of Congress
Prints and Photographs Section
Washington, DC 20540

Library of Congress
Superintendent of Documents
732 North Capitol Street, N.W.
Washington, DC 20401

MECC-Minn Educational Computing
    Corp.
Softkey International, Inc.
9715 Parkside Drive
Knoxville, TN 37922

Modern Curriculum Press
13900 Prospect Road
Cleveland, OH 44136

National Archives
Education Branch
Office of Public Programs
Washington, DC 20408

National Archives and Record Service
General Services Administration
Audiovisual Branch
Washington, DC 20408

National Association for the
   Education of Young Children
1509 16th Street, N.W.
Washington, DC 20036–1426

National Council for the Social
   Studies
3501 Newark Street, N.W.
Washington, DC 20016

National Gallery of Art
Department of Educational Resources
Washington, DC 20565

National Gallery of Art
Extension Services
Washington, DC 20565

National Genealogical Society
4527 17th Street North
Arlington, VA 22207-2399

National Geographic Society
1145 17th Street, N.W.
Washington, DC 20036-4688

National Museum of African Art
Department of Education, MRC 708
950 Independence Avenue, S.W.
Smithsonian Institution
Washington, DC 20560

National Museum of American Art
Office of Educational Programs,
   MRC 210
Smithsonian Institution
Washington, DC 20560

National Museum of American
   History
Division of Education
Room B1026, MRC 603
Smithsonian Institution
Washington, DC 20560

National Museum of American
   History
Division of Publications/Department
   of Public Programs
Room MBB-66, MRC 6456
Smithsonian Institution
Washington, DC 20560

National Museum of the American
   Indian
Publications Department
Smithsonian Institution
3753 Broadway at 155th Street
New York, NY 10032

National Register of Historic Places
Interagency Resources Division
National Park Service
U.S. Department of the Interior
P.O. Box 37127
Washington, DC 20013-7127

National Trust for Historic
   Preservation
1785 Massachusetts Avenue, N.W.
Washington, DC 20036

Native American Authors
   Distribution Project
The Greenfield Review Press
2 Middle Grove Road
P.O. Box 308
Greenfield Center, NY 12833

Native Voices Public Television
VCB Room 222
Montana State University
Bozeman, MT 59717

New World Records
701 Seventh Avenue
New York, NY 10036

New York Graphic Society
34 Beacon Street
Boston, MA 02108

Office of Elementary and Secondary
   Education
Smithsonian Institution
Arts and Industries Building
Room 1163, MRC 402
Washington, DC 20560

Office of Printing and Photographic
   Services
Smithsonian Institution
American History Building
Room CB-054, MRC 644
Washington, DC 20560

Oryx Press
4041 North Central Avenue
7th Floor
Phoenix, AZ 85012-3397

Oyate
2702 Mathews
Berkeley, CA 94702

Parks and History Association
P.O. Box 40060
Washington, DC 20016

Peace Links, Women Against
   Nuclear War
747 8th Street, S.E.
Washington, DC 20003

Penton Overseas
2091 Las Palmas Drive, Suite A
Carlsbad, CA 92009-1519

Phoenix/BFA Films and Video, Inc.
Department S1
468 Park Avenue South
New York, NY 10016

Pleasant Company Publications
P.O. Box 620991
Middleton, WI 53562-0991

Public Broadcasting Service
Public Affairs Information Service, Inc.
821 West 43rd Street
New York, NY 10036-5496

Recorded Books, Inc.
270 Skipjack
Prince Frederick, MD 20678

Schlessinger Video, Library Video
   Company
P.O. Box 1110
Department B
Bala-Cynwyd, PA 19004

Scholastic Inc.
P.O. Box 3710
Jefferson City, MO 65102

Smithsonian Books and Recordings
P.O. Box 2071
Colchester, VT 05449-0099

Smithsonian Information
Smithsonian Institution
S1 Building, Room 153, MRC 010
Washington, DC 20560

Social Studies School Series
10200 Jefferson Boulevard, Room R3
P.O. Box 802
Culver City, CA 90232-0802

SRA School Group
P.O. Box 543
Blacklick, OH 43004

Sundance Publishing Company
P.O. Box 1326
Littleton, MA 01460–0036

Teacher Idea Press
P.O. Box 6633
Englewood, CO 80155-6633

Teaching with Historic Places
National Register of Historic Places
National Park Service
P.O. Box 37127
Suite 250
Washington, DC 20013-7127

Third World Resources
464 19th Street
Oakland, CA 94612

Tom Snyder Productions
80 Coolidge Hill Road
Watertown, MA 02172

United States Committee for the
    United Nations Children's Fund
    (UNICEF)
333 East 38th Street
New York, NY 10016

United States Corps of Engineers
Army Map Service, Defense Mapping
    Agency
8613 Lee Highway
Fairfax, VA 22031-2137

Weekly Reader
443 Equity Drive
P.O. Box 16626
Columbus, OH 43216

WEM Records
16230 Van Buren Boulevard
Riverside, CA 92504

Youth Ambassadors
Department B
P.O. Box 5273
Bellingham, WA 98227

Zephyr Press
3316 Chapel North Avenue
Tucson, AZ 85728-6006

Professional Bibliography

B

ATWELL, NANCIE. 1987. *In the Middle*. Portsmouth, NH: Boynton/Cook.

This book for intermediate and middle school teachers demonstrates how departmentalized teachers support students as readers, writers, and thinkers. It gives teachers ideas for classroom organization, record-keeping and evaluation procedures, and teaching strategies.

CALKINS, LUCY M. 1994. *The Art of Teaching Writing*. Portsmouth, NH: Heinemann.

Calkins answers many questions about conducting a process writing classroom. In addition to ideas about writing workshops, she offers suggestions to help students write in content areas.

CORDEIRO, PAT. 1992. *Whole Learning: Whole Language and Content in the Upper Grades*. Katonah, NY: Richard C. Owen.

Cordeiro explains how whole language integrates various areas of the curriculum in intermediate classrooms. She shows how subjects can revolve around the same theme or concept.

———. 1995. *Endless Possibilities: Generating Curriculum in Social Studies and Literacy*. Portsmouth, NH: Heinemann.

Teachers tell with their own voices about what it means to generate curriculum. Cordeiro gives examples showing how students share the responsibility and enjoyment of learning.

DANIELS, HARVEY. 1994. *Literature Circles: Voice and Choice in the Student Centered Classroom*. York, ME: Stenhouse.

Literature circles provide a way to organize the discussion of children's books that students read independently. Daniels shows teachers how to use literature circles with cooperative learning techniques.

ERNST, KAREN. 1994. *Picturing Learning: Artists and Writers in the Classroom*. Portsmouth, NH: Heinemann.

Ernst explains how to integrate art into all areas of the curriculum. The description of the artists' workshop reveals how to help students use a variety of media to express their thoughts and ideas.

FARRIS, PAMELA, and SUSAN COOPER. 1994. *Elementary Social Studies: A Whole Language Approach*. Dubuque, IA: William. C. Brown.

Farris and Cooper look at the social studies curriculum in a whole language classroom. They include chapters on technology, multiculturalism, bilingualism, inclusion, and many more issues plus many print and non-print resources.

GAMBERG, RUTH, WINNIEFRED KWAK, MEREDITH HUTCHINGS, and JUDY ALTHEIM. 1988. *Learning and Loving It: Theme Studies in the Classroom*. Portsmouth, NH: Heinemann.

The authors define theme studies and share the guidelines they use in selecting a theme and identifying resources. Actual classroom case studies illustrate the practical applications of a theme study.

GRAVES, DONALD. 1989. *Investigate Nonfiction*. Portsmouth, NH: Heinemann.

Graves provides excellent suggestions for students engaging in nonfiction writing. Teachers learn how to help students find information through interviewing, researching, and recording data and then turning the information into well-written nonfiction.

———. 1994. *A Fresh Look at Writing*. Portsmouth, NH: Heinemann.

This comprehensive guide to implementing a process writing classroom is complete with information on every aspect of supporting students as they become writers. It is helpful for language arts teachers and teachers of any discipline.

HAYDEN, CARLA D., ed. 1992. *Venture into Cultures: A Resource Book of Multicultural Materials and Programs*. Chicago: American Library Association.

This is a resource book about various cultures found in significant numbers in the United States, including African, Asian, Hispanic, Jewish, Persian, and Native American cultures. It includes annotated bibliographies of children's books and other materials for learning about ethnic groups.

LINDQUIST, TARRY. 1995. *Seeing the Whole Through Social Studies*. Portsmouth, NH: Heinemann.

Lindquist, a fifth-grade classroom teacher, takes the reader through an entire year of an integrated curriculum. She describes and explains the structure and purpose of her holistic learning experiences.

MANNING, MARYANN, GARY MANNING, and ROBERTA LONG. 1994. *Theme Immersion: Inquiry-Based Curriculum in Elementary and Middle Schools*. Portsmouth, NH: Heinemann.

The theme immersion process helps a teacher develop a generative curriculum. Guided engagement, assessment and evaluation, and many other aspects of theme immersions are addressed.

PETERSON, RALPH. 1992. *Life in a Crowded Place*. Portsmouth, NH: Heinemann.

Every classroom teacher needs to read this book; it shows how to build learning communities. Peterson offers a framework for the development of a caring place as he discusses ceremonies, rituals, rites, and celebrations.

RIEF, LINDA. 1992. *Seeking Diversity*. Portsmouth, NH: Heinemann.

Rief explains how she teaches adolescents in a departmentalized classroom to read, write, and think. She shows how she uses the life experiences of students to engage them in becoming better readers and writers.

ROUTMAN, REGIE. 1994. *Invitations*. Portsmouth, NH: Heinemann.

Routman includes excellent strategies that can be used to develop literate students. The comprehensive volume includes the Blue Pages section, which contains an annotated bibliography of trade books. The Blue Pages have been updated and published as a separate volume.

SHORT, KATHY, JEROME C. HARSTE, and CAROLYN BURKE. 1995. *Creating Classrooms for Authors and Inquirers*. Portsmouth, NH: Heinemann.

The authors explain how teachers create literacy-learning environments; they present descriptions of classrooms and ideas that help students become readers, writers, and inquirers.

SHORT, KATHY G., et al. 1996. *Learning Together Through Inquiry*. York, ME: Stenhouse.

Short and others explain the inquiry cycle and negotiated curriculum. They show how it is possible to move from a textbook-based curriculum to thematic units to inquiry approaches.

SLAPIN, BEVERLY, and DORIS SEALE, eds. 1992. *Through Indian Eyes: The Native American Experience in Books for Children*. Berkeley, CA: New Society/Oyate.

The authors point out racism and bias in books with Native American characters. The book includes checklists for evaluating children's books about Native Americans, a bibliography, and lists of resources and curriculum materials.

Steffey, Stephanie, and Wendy Hood, eds. 1994. *If This Is Social Studies, Why Isn't It Boring?* York, ME: Stenhouse.

Each chapter is written by a classroom teacher who discusses strategies that brought social studies alive in the elementary and secondary school.

Tunnel, Michael O., and Richard Ammons, eds. 1993. *The Story of Ourselves: Teaching History Through Children's Literature.* Portsmouth, NH: Heinemann.

Guidance and suggestions for teachers who want to use children's literature in their social studies programs are given. In addition to the practical suggestions for bringing history alive with children's books, there is a comprehensive bibliography of trade books about North American history.

Whitin, David, and Phylis Whitin. 1997. *Inquiry at the Window: Pursuing the Wonders of Learners.* Portsmouth, NH: Heinemann.

A valuable resource for preservice and inservice elementary teachers who want a close look at interdisciplinary learning.

Young, Katherine A. 1994. *Constructing Buildings, Bridges and Minds: Building an Integrated Curriculum Through Social Studies.* Portsmouth, NH: Heinemann.

Young offers a conceptual framework for integrating the curriculum around social studies. She explains how students become problem-solvers as they work together improving their thinking, reading, writing, and speaking.

Resources for Evaluation

Student Self-Evaluation of Discussion in Groups

Check Yes, No, or Sometimes	Yes	No	Sometimes
1. Can you define a problem or issue?	____	____	____
2. Can you state clearly your views about a problem or issue?	____	____	____
3. Do you know how to find the facts?	____	____	____
4. Can you identify relevant information?	____	____	____
5. Do you believe you can be objective about all issues?	____	____	____
6. Do you know how to present persuasive evidence for your point of view?	____	____	____
7. Do you listen to everyone's point of view?	____	____	____
8. Do you respect the opinions of others?	____	____	____
9. Do you monopolize the discussions or take your turn?	____	____	____
10. Can you find the underlying values of a position?	____	____	____
11. Can you consider the consequences of a position?	____	____	____
12. Can you consider the monetary cost of a position?	____	____	____
13. Do you consider alternative positions?	____	____	____
14. Do you change your mind if you find that your position is weak or wrong?	____	____	____
15. Are you willing to become informed about alternative positions?	____	____	____
16. Can you make compromises in order to reach an agreement?	____	____	____
17. Can you put yourself in a policy-making position?	____	____	____

Student Self-Evaluation of Project

Check Yes, No, or Sometimes	Yes	No	Sometimes
Did I use my time effectively			
at school?	_____	_____	_____
at home?	_____	_____	_____
Did I develop a personal timeline to help me complete my work?	_____	_____	_____
Did I complete the work according to the timeline?	_____	_____	_____
Did I use a variety of sources?	_____	_____	_____
Can I generate a number of ideas?	_____	_____	_____
Can I develop my ideas with depth?	_____	_____	_____
Do I think about problems and issues in different ways?	_____	_____	_____
Do I explore and present ideas in unique ways?	_____	_____	_____

I used the following sources:

_____

_____

_____

_____

I accomplished the following things:

_____

_____

_____

_____

If I were grading my own project, I would give it the following grade:_____

State your reasons for the grade:

_____

_____

_____

Student Self-Evaluation of Group Work

Name _____

Name of group _____ Date _____

During this past week while working on the _____
(report/project), I especially appreciate _____
for _____

I experienced conflict with a group member.   yes   no
If you marked yes, how did you resolve the conflict?

_____
_____

What I liked best was _____

_____
_____

What I would have changed about the group's activity was

_____
_____
_____

Resources I used this week were _____

_____
_____

Resources that gave me the most information were _____

_____
_____

As a result of my research, I think my question/issue is (or isn't)
important because _____

_____
_____

I would give my group's work (project, report, etc.) a grade of

_____

Theme Immersion Rubric

Name _____Date _____

Characteristics	Yes	No	Sometimes
1. Shows intellectual curiosity by developing questions related to topic/issue	_____	_____	_____
2. Works cooperatively with other group members	_____	_____	_____
3. Uses a variety of resources other than the encyclopedia	_____	_____	_____
4. Records notes when reading and organizes notes before writing or speaking	_____	_____	_____
5. Listens attentively to media, resource people, teacher, and others	_____	_____	_____
6. Participates actively in group discussions	_____	_____	_____
7. Listens to other points of view and tries to be objective	_____	_____	_____
8. Uses available technology to access information and solve problems	_____	_____	_____
9. Increases knowledge about topics	_____	_____	_____
10. Completes individual and group work within time frame	_____	_____	_____
11. Final products (if written) show content and mechanics revisions	_____	_____	_____

Final Grade_____

_____

A—yes for almost all areas (at least 10 of 11)

B—yes/sometimes for most areas (at least 8 of 11)

C—yes/sometimes for many areas (at least 6 of 11)

D—yes/sometimes for some areas (at least 5 of 11)

F—yes/sometimes for few areas (4 or fewer of 11)

Student Portfolio Checklist

1. Is every entry in the portfolio dated?

2. Are all the portfolio contents appropriate?

3. Are there samples that show that I have learned something new?

4. Are there samples that indicate how my research abilities are improving?

5. Are there samples that indicate that my writing ability is increasing?

6. Are there samples of work that was difficult and work that was easy?

7. Are there samples that show creativity and originality?

8. Does each sample have a self-evaluation of the work?

9. Are published works neat?

Evaluation of Student Portfolios

Check Yes or No	Yes	No
Does the portfolio include self-assessments of the following items?		
Discussion	_____	_____
Reading	_____	_____
Research	_____	_____
Project presentation	_____	_____
Writing	_____	_____
Does the portfolio contain information that documents the following?		
Contributions to group projects	_____	_____
Community service	_____	_____
Future learning goals	_____	_____
Summaries of learning history	_____	_____
Peer assessments	_____	_____
Teacher comments	_____	_____
Parent comments	_____	_____
Principal comments	_____	_____
Are there samples of the student's work in the portfolio?		
Drafts, revisions, and published work	_____	_____
Journal entries	_____	_____
Different genres, including:	_____	_____
Letters	_____	_____
Logs	_____	_____
Poems	_____	_____
Reflections	_____	_____
Research notes	_____	_____
Photographs	_____	_____
Audiotapes of reports, etc.	_____	_____
Videotapes of activities	_____	_____
Visual artwork	_____	_____
Sketches of projects	_____	_____

[Note: Most of the items suggested for the evaluation of individual portfolios can also be used for the evaluation of group portfolios. The following are additional ideas that can be used to evaluate the group portfolio: lists from brainstorming sessions; notes from discussions; weekly progress reports; and samples of group work.]

Questions for Students to Use in Evaluating Texts

Where was the text published?

What was the original medium (newspaper, government document, letter)?

Who is the author's intended audience?

Is the information accurate?

Are there omissions in the information?

Why do you think the author wrote about the topic?

Is the author an authority on the topic?

What is the author's specialized knowledge or expertise?

Is the author's perspective logical?

Do other sources support the author's perspective?

Are the voices the author portrays authentic?

Are any of the author's words confusing?

Did the author use any loaded words? If so, which ones and why?

Is the author biased?

Does the author have a hidden agenda?

Did the author use any propaganda techniques?

Student Self-Evaluation of Written Work

	Yes	No
Content		
Does each sentence say what I want it to say?	_____	_____
Do the sentences need to be reworded to better express my ideas?	_____	_____
Are there better words to use?	_____	_____
Do my sentences link to one another?	_____	_____
Do my paragraphs link to one another?	_____	_____
Are my thoughts in logical order?	_____	_____
Does the piece make sense?	_____	_____
Are there any words left out?	_____	_____
Are there any important ideas left out?	_____	_____
Are there any words that are used too often?	_____	_____
Is there content redundancy in the piece?	_____	_____
Mechanics		
Are the words spelled correctly?	_____	_____
Is the punctuation correct?	_____	_____
Can others read the writing?	_____	_____
Is the paper neat?	_____	_____
Bibliography		
Did I list all sources that were used in my research?	_____	_____
Is the information about the sources correct?	_____	_____
Is the information complete?	_____	_____
Is the style of each entry correct?	_____	_____
Final Published Piece		
Can others read my handwriting?	_____	_____
Is the spacing of the page proportioned?	_____	_____
Does each page look neat?	_____	_____

Self-Evaluation of Published Writing or Finished Project

Answer the following questions about your published writing or finished project.

How much time did you spend on the published writing or finished project?_____

_____

_____

What did you try to improve? _____

_____

_____

What is the best part? _____

_____

_____

What are the strengths of the published writing or finished project?

_____

_____

What are the weaknesses? _____

_____

_____

What will you do differently on your next published writing or finished project?_____

_____

_____

Evaluation by Parents

Child's name _____

Parent completing form _____

Check Yes, No, or Sometimes	Yes	No	Sometimes
My child keeps me informed about the topic of the theme immersion.	____	____	____
My child reads in the evening and on the weekends on the theme immersion topic.	____	____	____
My child occasionally tells me about the content of the theme immersion topic.	____	____	____
My child involves me in finding information about the theme immersion topic.	____	____	____
My child is decreasing the amount of time watching television, and is now watching some educational television.	____	____	____
My child is improving in his/her ability to read and write.	____	____	____
My child is increasing his/her ability to take notes.	____	____	____
My child is increasing his/her confidence in asking others for information about a topic being researched.	____	____	____

Comments:

_____

_____

_____

_____

_____

_____

Teacher Self-Evaluation

Check Yes, No, or Sometimes	Yes	No	Sometimes
Can my students define and state problems or issues?	_____	_____	_____
Are my students learning to make decisions about those issues/problems with which they agree and disagree?	_____	_____	_____
Are my students growing in their ability to inquire?	_____	_____	_____
Are my students becoming more competent as they conduct searches for information?	_____	_____	_____
Are my students learning to use technology to find information and to find solutions to problems?	_____	_____	_____
Are my students using a variety of resources to answer questions?	_____	_____	_____
Are my students growing in their ability to examine their research findings?	_____	_____	_____
Are my students increasing their ability to organize their research findings?	_____	_____	_____
Are my students becoming more objective as they weigh different problems?	_____	_____	_____
Are my students becoming open to considering opposing points of view?	_____	_____	_____
Are my students deliberating their choices before making decisions?	_____	_____	_____
Are my students becoming more able to present their research findings verbally, in writing, and through displays?	_____	_____	_____

Letters to Parents

Beginning of the Year Letter

Dear _____,

Throughout the year your child will be engaged in many TIs (theme immersions). The term may be new to you, but you are probably familiar with the concept.

A theme immersion is an in-depth study of one topic or issue in which the students take responsibility for some of their learning. I am using theme immersions because numerous educational studies have shown that students who have responsibility for choosing some of the topics they study are more interested in learning. Also, if students choose some of the methods by which they find the information, they will become more independent in their learning.

During the year you might support your child's learning in many different ways. Please consider the following:

- Be aware of the TI your child is studying.
- Ask your child to tell you what he/she has learned and the questions he/she is researching.
- Help your child find the answers to questions at home or by taking him/her to the public library.
- Take your child to places in the community that relate to the topic being studied.
- Arrange for your child to interview someone you know who is knowledgeable about the topic.
- Help find resource people who can speak to the class on the topic.

I look forward to working with you this year. Please make me aware of anything I can do to increase your child's learning.

Sincerely yours,

Beginning of the Theme Immersion Letter

Dear _____,

Our class is beginning a theme immersion on _____.
We need your help as we study this topic. There are several ways you can help, including the following:

- Tell your child what you know about the topic.
- Find books, videos, or software about the topic and study the materials with your child.
- Locate objects or pictures about the topic in your home or community.
- Let me know about community activities that relate to the topic.
- Let me know about area sites that could serve as class field trips or family outings.
- Volunteer to help in the classroom with projects.
- Volunteer to pick up materials or resource people from the community.

Thank you for considering any one of these important activities.

Sincerely,

Student Aids for Research

Steps in Conducting Research

Step 1: Begin with a question that you have asked relating to the subtopic of your study. Make sure the question is specific.

Step 2: Look for information to answer the question.

- Refer to the Research Sources to help you think about all of the possibilities.
- Use a variety of sources, including a computer search.

Step 3: Consult with others to find appropriate information.

- Ask your teacher, the librarian, and family members.
- Write letters to others through regular mail or the Internet.

Step 4: Gather information through the sources.

- Read, observe, and/or listen carefully.
- Take notes. Summarize what you read. If you copy any information, put it in quotation marks so you can paraphrase or keep the quote when you write.
- Be persistent in your search for answers.

Step 5: Record the sources you use for your bibliography on cards so you can alphabetize them.

Step 6: Determine the way you are going to present your information. (See the Presentation Strategies in this appendix for possibilities.)

Step 7: Organize the research so that it is presented in a logical and coherent manner.

Step 8: Create the project. If the form of presentation is a written research paper, for example, you will write the first draft.

Step 9: Rework the project. If it is a research paper, you will revise and edit the work.

Step 10: Finalize the project. If it is a research paper, you will publish the paper.

Step 11: Critique your final product and the processes you used as a researcher.

Research Sources

Books
Anthropology
Autobiography
Biography
Fiction
Geography
History
Legends
Myths
Natural science
Nonfiction
Physical science
Poetry
Political science

Experiences
Demonstrations
Experiments
Family vacations
Field trips
Laboratory
Observation museums
Touch

Media
Films
Filmstrips

Microfilms
Radio
Slides
Tape recorder
Television
Videodiscs
Videos

Newspapers and Magazines
Book, movie, play reviews
Cartoons
Editorials
Feature articles
Financial sections
Narratives in magazines
Political news—local, state, national, international
Stock market reports
Want ads
Weather reports

Primary Sources
Architecture
Artifacts
Buildings
Business ledgers
Cemetery records
Church records
Clothing
Coins
Cornerstones
Court documents
Diaries
Family documents
Government documents
Historical markers
Interviews
Journals
Letters
Logs
Memoirs
Military records
Monuments
Organizational records
Paintings

Photographs
Plaques
Record books
Relics
Ruins
Samples
Speeches
Surveys
Telephone conversations
Tools

Reference Materials
Almanacs
Atlases
Bibliographies
Biographies
Encyclopedias
Histories
Textbooks

Symbolic Sources
Blueprints
Calendars
Cartoons
Census records
Diagrams
Formulas
Globes
Graphs
Illustrations
Maps
Models
Music
Photographs
Scales
Thermometers
Topographical sketches
Works of art

Technology
CD-ROM
Computer programs
Hypertext
World Wide Web

Taking Notes

Topic: _____

Aspect of topic: _____ Copyright date: _____

Source: _____

Author(s): _____

Notes: _____

_____

_____

_____

_____

_____

_____

_____

_____

_____

Topic: _____

Aspect of topic: _____ Copyright date: _____

Source: _____

Author(s): _____

Notes: _____

_____

_____

_____

_____

_____

_____

_____

_____

Developing a Bibliography

A bibliography is a list of sources used when studying a topic. There are many different styles for developing a bibliography. We provide examples of one style.

Books

Author. date. *Title of Book*. City, State: Publisher.

Sullivan, A. 1982. *Thirty Important Battles of the Revolutionary War*. Spring Hill, TN: Bearden Press.

Computer Programs

Author or Editor. date. *Title (edition)*, Type of medium. Producer [optional]. Supplier or Database Name. Database Identifier or Number [if available]. Item or Accession Number. (Accession date).

Kelava, I. 1997. *War in Bosnia* (v1.0), Computer Program. Cathedral River Inc. (Accessed 1977, January 10).

Encyclopedias

Editors [if stated]. date. *Title*. City, State: Publisher.

Fernandez, C., ed. 1989. *Encyclopedia of Nations*. Newark, NJ: Wilson Publishers.

Interviews

Interviewer. date of interview. Interview with name of person, title of person.

Novak, C. March 9, 1985. Interview with Mary Person, chairperson of Pioneer Society.

Newspaper Articles

"Title of article." date. *Newspaper*, page number.

"Cuban Immigrants Picnic." July 7, 1984. *Madison Times*, p. B5.

Periodicals (Articles from Magazines)

Author. date. "Title of Article." *Name of Journal/Magazine volume number*, pages.

Olive, K. 1966. "Reading Science Texts and Finding Details." *Education: Tips for Students 3*, 8–10.

Personal Communications

Name of person writing letter. (Personal communication, date).

Dederman, M. (Personal communication, July 1996).

Recordings

Speaker's name (narrator). Date of Recording. *Title of Recording* number if series. City, State where recording was made: Company.

Valentine, J. (narrator). 1993. *Great Battles of the Revolutionary* War No. 24. Norfolk, IA: Percy Recording Company.

Unpublished Materials and Personal Files

Author. date. [Type of Material]. Source.

Booker, B. 1863. [Civil War Diary]. Unpublished diary.

Videos, Films, Filmstrips

Producer and Director. (date medium was made). *Title* (type of media). City, State where medium was made: Company that made the medium.

James, H. (producer) and Hampton, B. (director). 1993. *Forty Famous English Americans* (video). Columbus, VA: Heritage Videos.

Conducting an Interview with a Resource Person

It is important to identify people who have knowledge about the subject you are researching. Once you have identified a person who is willing to be interviewed, you must prepare for the interview. The following steps will help you plan and conduct a successful interview.

Before the Interview

1. Contact the person to ask for an appointment for the interview.
   - State the purpose of the interview in a clear and polite manner.
   - Ask the person for the times when he/she is available.
   - Ask the person to suggest the best place for the interview: at home, business, or school.
   - Ask if you may audiotape or videotape the interview.
2. Develop a list of questions for the interview.
   - Ask the questions that will obtain the information you are seeking.
   - Ask a question in different ways so you can secure a more complete response.
3. Gather the supplies for the interview.
   - Obtain a release form for tape recording or videotaping.
   - Collect paper, sketch pads, pencils, and camera.

- Obtain audiotape and tape recorder or videotape and video recorder, if you are recording the interview.
- Ask a friend to accompany you, if you are recording, so she/he can help with the recording.

During the Interview

1. Greet the person in a warm manner. If the person is not too busy, engage in casual conversation for a few minutes.
2. Ask the person to sign a release form so you can audiotape or videotape the interview.
3. Ask the person questions from your prepared list, but ask other questions based on what the person says.
4. Take notes, even if you are taping the interview, in case your equipment fails.
5. Close the interview by thanking the person for his/her time. If pamphlets, brochures, or other printed materials are referred to in the interview, ask if you may have or borrow a copy. If a camera is available, ask for permission to take a photograph.

After the Interview

1. Write a report on the interview, which should include an introduction, a summary of information learned from the interviewee, and a conclusion.
2. Use statements from the audio- or videotape recording.
3. Write a thank you note or letter thanking the person for his/her time and other courtesies.

Release Form for Audio- or Videotaping

I give _____ permission to (circle one of the following): audiotape videotape the interview that will be conducted with me on _____. I understand that the tape will be used for documentation purposes and will be used only by students in _____school.

Signed _____ Date _____

Oral History Through Interviews

Interviewing is an important and interesting way to collect oral history information about an event or person from someone who has firsthand knowledge. In so doing, you will create a primary source for yourself and others.

Consider gathering the information with another student. As you work together, you will be able to help each other with every phase of the project.

The interview can be conducted at your school or perhaps at the person's home or business. It is important that you and the person you are interviewing feel comfortable with the interview setting.

Initial Steps

1. Identify the event or person you want to know more about.
2. Identify a person who has firsthand knowledge about the event or person.
3. Make an appointment with the person.
4. Determine where and when the interview will occur.
5. Develop the questions you will ask in the interview. Your teacher, classmates, parents, and others should be helpful as you develop questions. Arrange the questions in a logical order and conduct a mock interview.
6. Make certain you have the necessary materials, such as an audio- or videotape recorder, paper, pencils, notebook, extension cord, camera, and sketch pads.

Interview

1. If you plan to tape record, ask the person for permission. If the person agrees, ask him/her to sign the release form. If you are recording, check your equipment to determine if it is working.
2. Ask the person to give his/her name and begin with background information about the event or person.
3. Try to be flexible in the way you ask questions, rather than following one question after another in a rigid manner.
4. Ask the person if you may take photographs to include with a transcription of the interview.
5. Find out if the person you are interviewing has any possessions that will help with your research, such as a bill of sale, newspaper clippings, clothing, diaries, or letters.
6. Complete the interview within one hour. If you need more information, ask if you may have a second interview.
7. Thank the person for his/her time.

Compile the Information

1. Write a thank-you letter.
2. Transcribe the audio- or videotape. Summarize the notes that you took during the interview.
3. Write a report of the interview and present it to the class.
4. Offer a copy of the tapes, notes, and final project to the school library and/or local historical society.

Release Form

I give permission for the audiotape or videotape (circle one) and/or transcription of my interview to be placed on file in a library or other appropriate place. I understand that the interview will not be used for commercial purposes.

Signature_____Date_____

Oral History Bibliography

ANDERSON, JOAN. 1988. *From Map to Museum: Uncovering Mysteries of the Past*. New York: Morrow.

BROWN, CYNTHIA S. 1988. *Like It Was: A Complete Guide to Writing Oral History*. New York: Teachers and Writers Collaborative.

COOPER, KAY. 1985. *Who Put the Cannon in the Courthouse Square?: A Guide to Uncovering the Past*. New York: Walker.

LEVIN, BETTY. 1981. *The Keeping Room*. New York: Greenwillow.

LOEPER, JOHN J. 1982. *The House on Spruce Street*. New York: Atheneum.

PERL, LILA. 1989. *The Great Ancestor Hunt: The Fun of Finding Out Who You Are*. New York: Clarion.

VON TSCHARNER, RENATA, RONALD LEE FLEMING, et al. 1987. *New Providence: A Changing Cityscape*. San Diego: Harcourt Brace Jovanovich.

WEITZMAN, DAVID. 1975. *My Backyard History Book*. Boston: Little, Brown.

WOLFMAN, IRA. 1991a. *Do People Grow on Family Trees?* New York: Workman Publishers.

———. 1991b. *Genealogy for Kids and other Beginners*. New York: Workman Publishers.

———. 1991c. *The Official Ellis Island Handbook*. New York: Workman Publishers.

Researching Family History

Researching your own family history is interesting and rewarding. Through family history, you develop personal links with your ancestors, making history come alive.

Steps to Follow

1. Develop a genealogical chart of your family. Ask older family members to help you collect the names of ancestors and other information: occupations, ethnicity, education, and places where they lived.

2. Interview family members. If possible, audiotape or videotape the interviews.

   Begin the interview by asking your relative to give his/her name, birth date and place, his/her parents' names, and other information he/she wishes to share.

   Prepare questions to ask of your relative, but do not be concerned if you do not ask all of the questions in the first interview. Sample questions might include:

   - What is your nationality?
   - What work did your mother and father do?
   - Did you go into the same occupation as your mother or father? Why or why not?
   - How many days each week did your parents work?
   - Where did your family live when you were a child?
   - What was your home like as a child?
   - Did your grandparents live with you? If not, where did they live? Why?
   - Where did people sleep in your home when you were a child?
   - Who did the household work?
   - How were clothes washed?
   - Who cooked the food? What kinds of food did you eat?
   - What did the family do for recreation?
   - Did other family members live near you?
   - What toys did you have as a child?
   - What did teenagers do for fun?
   - How much schooling did you complete? Why?
   - What were some family celebrations?
   - What were family customs when someone died? married?
   - How far back can you trace your family? What can you tell me about your ancestors?
   - What work did women and men do in the home?
   - What stories do you know about older family members?

- Do you have any photos of older family members? If so, may I see them and will you tell me what you know about them?
- Do you have any family artifacts such as uniforms, flags, or jewelry? If so, may I see them and will you tell me what you know about them? (Consider asking to photograph the artifacts.)

3. Summarize and share your research. Transcribe video or audio recordings and write reports about family history, using direct quotes from the transcriptions and/or your notes. Include a description of physical and personality traits. Publish family history in a form such as a booklet that can be easily reproduced for interested family members. Offer your published family history to other groups such as a library or historical society.

Guidelines for Writing a Business Letter

The purposes of a business letter related to a TI are:
- To request information
- To request printed materials
- To arrange for a resource person to speak to the class
- To thank a resource person for speaking to the class
- To arrange for an interview
- To thank a person for an interview

The contents of a business letter should be:
- Concise
- Courteous
- Specific
- Inclusive

The parts of a business letter are:
- Heading (return address and date)
- Inside address (name and address of person to whom the letter is being sent)
- Salutation (title and name of person)
- Body (the letter itself)
- Closing (a word such as "Sincerely")
- Signature (first and last name of person sending the letter)

Following is an example of a complete business letter and two letter bodies:

Requesting a Brochure

Oakmont School
30 Hightower Road
Hubbell, Nebraska 69970
April 23, 1996

Mrs. Lydia Douglas, President
Peace Institute of America
641 Elmore Parkway, Suite 18
Park City, CA 90232

Dear Mrs. Douglas:

My fifth-grade class is conducting a theme immersion on world peace. During our research, we found information about your organization that stated that you have a free brochure on promoting world peace.

Please know that my classmates and teacher are genuinely interested in world peace. We will be grateful to you if you send us a brochure.

Sincerely,
[student's name]

Inviting a Speaker

Our class at Dunbar Middle School is engaged in a theme immersion on the settlement of Arkansas. Your name has been given to our class by John Wallace, a guide at the Marymount Historical Society. He stated that you have collected information about early settlers in this area of Arkansas between 1850 and 1900.

We invite you to speak to our class at your earliest convenience. Our theme immersion time is scheduled in the afternoon between 1:00 and 3:00, but we can make arrangements for any time that is convenient for you.

We hope you will consider our request to speak on any school day. Please call or fax me or my teacher, Mr. Underbakke, at the school. The telephone number is 837-2453 and the fax number is 837-9681. Thank you for considering our request.

Thanking a Speaker

Thank you for taking time from your busy schedule to speak to our class. The information you presented on the Civil War was very interesting. We also appreciated seeing the artifacts you shared with the class. Because of the interest you created in Civil War music, several students are researching Civil War songs.

In closing, we again thank you for sharing your expertise with our class. You inspired students to study the topic of the Civil War with vigor and enthusiasm.

Editing Checklist

Content
Is the content accurate?
Is the writing clear?
Does it say what I want it to say?
Are there sentences or paragraphs that need to be reworded?
Are paragraphs and sentences linked together?
Does the piece sound right?
Are there any ideas left out that should be included?
Is the same information stated more than once in the piece?
Are some words used too often?

Mechanics
Are all the sentences complete?
Did I use correct grammar?
Are all proper nouns, titles, and trade names capitalized?
Did I use correct punctuation?
Are all words spelled correctly?

Bibliography
Did I list all sources that were used in my research?
Is the information about the sources correct?
Is the information complete?
Is the style of each entry correct?

Final Published Copy
Can others read my writing?
Is the spacing of the page appropriate?
Does each page look neat and well organized?

Making an Oral Presentation

Follow these steps when making an individual or group oral presentation.

1. Decide on the information you want to present to the class. Include important and relevant information.

2. Outline your information to make sure the information is presented in a logical and organized manner.

3. Decide on your presentation strategy. (Refer to the list of presentation strategies below.) You may want to use more than one strategy in your presentation.

4. Prepare the presentation. Consider using visual aids to enhance the quality of the presentation.

5. Practice making the presentation. Ask someone else to critique the presentation, making suggestions to improve it.

6. Evaluate the suggestions that were made and incorporate those ideas, if you agree with them.

7. Rehearse the presentation using props and visual aids.

8. Make your presentation knowing that you are fully prepared.

9. After you have given the presentation, reflect on what you would do differently or the same. Ask others who were in the audience to critique your presentation.

Presentation Strategies

Art
Bulletin boards
Collage
Costume
Etchings
Illustrations
Mobiles
Murals
Photographic essays
Placemats
Posters
Scrolls
Signs
Sketches
Watercolors

Drama
Improvisations
Mime
Monologues
News broadcasts
Plays
Puppet plays
Radio scripts
Simulations
Skits
Telephone dialogues
Trials

Literary Styles
Advertisements
Articles in newspapers or magazines
Art reviews
Biographies

Booklets
Brochures
Character analyses
Children's books
Class books
Diaries
Dictionaries
Dust jackets
Editorials
Essays
Eyewitness accounts
Fables
Fairy tales
Flashbacks
Interview reports
Jokes
Legends
Letters (formal, friendly, personal, to editor)
Lists of facts
Narratives
Newscasts
Newsletters
Obituaries
Opinion pieces
Pamphlets
Parallel nursery rhymes
Poems
Prose pieces
Questionnaires
Raps
Research papers
Stories
Written conversations
Written debates

Media
Audio- and videotapes
Computer programs
Filmstrips
Overhead transparencies
Photographs
Slides
Slide tape presentations
Video productions
World Wide Web pages

Music
Commercial jingles
Operas
Song lyrics

Speech Forms
Audience participation
Debates
Demonstrations
Discussions
Flannel board story
Monologues
Oral reports
Panel discussions
Persuasion speeches
Readers' theater

Symbolic Presentations
Calendars
Cartoons
Charts
Diagrams
Graphs
Lab reports/observations
Maps
Mobiles

Three-Dimensional
Constructions
Dioramas
Sculptures
Shadow boxes

Other
Bingo game
Board game